CW01500396

YOSHUKU

YOSHUKU

The Japanese
Art of Manifesting

AZUMI UCHITANI

MICHAEL JOSEPH

PENGUIN MICHAEL JOSEPH

UK | USA | Canada | Ireland | Australia
India | New Zealand | South Africa

Penguin Michael Joseph is part of the Penguin Random House group of companies
whose addresses can be found at global.penguinrandomhouse.com.

Penguin Random House UK
One Embassy Gardens, 8 Viaduct Gardens, London SW11 7BW

penguin.co.uk

First published 2025

002

Set in 12.5/18pt Bembo Book MT Pro
Typeset by Jouve (UK), Milton Keynes
Printed and bound in Great Britain by Clays Ltd, Elcograf S.p.A.

The authorized representative in the EEA is Penguin Random House Ireland,
Morrison Chambers, 32 Nassau Street, Dublin D02 YH68

A CIP catalogue record for this book is available from the British Library.

ISBN: 978-0-241-72623-5

Penguin Random House is committed to a sustainable future
for our business, our readers and our planet. This book is made from
Forest Stewardship Council® certified paper.

To my son, Max –
my greatest gift, my shining light.

Contents

Prologue: Typhoons and Cherry Blossom   ix

Part 1: The Wisdom of Yoshuku

  1. What is Yoshuku?   3

  2. Cultivating Healthy Roots   19

  3. Why Pre-Celebration Brings Manifestation   27

  4. The Power of Yoshuku   43

Part 2: The Practice of Yoshuku

  Create Your Own Yoshuku   79

  Step 1: Cultivate Your Wish   89

  Step 2: Mind-Preparation   99

  Step 3: Planning and Creating Your
      Yoshuku Celebrations   109

  Step 4: Daily Rituals   143

  Step 5: Honouring the Journey   183

Epilogue   191

Godai – The Five Elements of Life   193

Glossary   195

Acknowledgements   207

Sakura

cherry blossom

Prologue:
Typhoons and Cherry Blossom

I have always held close the wisdom I learned from our family's Buddhist monk.

I was born and raised in a traditional family in Wakayama, a land where nature and spirituality are deeply intertwined. This region, with its breathtaking landscapes of sea and mountains, is dotted with sacred sites such as Mount Koya – the long-ago birthplace of Shingon Buddhism – and home to the ancient pilgrimage route of Kumano Kodo, which people travel to worship nature and the deities of the natural world in Shinto tradition. Growing up in such a setting has profoundly shaped my path and my understanding of life.

My childhood was enriched with celebrations and rituals rooted in Shinto and Buddhism. One of the most important of these events is O-Bon, a traditional Buddhist event to honour and heal the spirit of our ancestors, which families and communities celebrate together every August. Each O-Bon, a Buddhist monk comes to perform a special ceremony for my family and ancestors, and to this day I try to return home to be present for it. In this later part of the summer, however, Wakayama is often hit by typhoons, a vivid reminder of nature's uncontrollable power. One year, the monk's ceremony coincided with a heavy storm. After his long prayer, delivered against the sounds of the raging wind and rain outside, the monk sipped his tea and said calmly, 'Remember, next spring we will have beautiful *sakura* cherry blossom. Do you know why? During heavy storms like typhoons, the trees endure; they are invigorated and develop more roots to survive. When the trees become stronger, with more vital energy, they give more blossom in the spring.'

And I have learned that this is true for us humans, too. While we are on our journeys to blossom and manifest our dreams, we may face hardship and feel like giving up. But these are opportunities for invigoration and growth. We become stronger in spirit, and blossom all the more abundantly for it. It is a part of our journey to make our dreams come true.

In my early twenties, moving from Japan to England to pursue my studies before settling in Amsterdam, I set goals and had a wish list, as many of us do. One by one, I manifested everything I wanted. By the age of twenty-five, I had bought a house and got married; I started my first business at twenty-nine and became a mother at thirty-one. By thirty-two, my life was abundant in material wealth. However, alongside this prosperity, I was plagued by a chronic autoimmune disorder. I masked my physical and mental suffering and continued manifesting the life of luxury I shared with my husband at that time. What we achieved together – his career, my career – all looked glorious from the outside, but inside I was suffering, and my marriage was falling apart.

And then came the typhoon of my life: I found myself on the brink of death in hospital.

In the abyss of darkness, I experienced *satori*, a sudden enlightenment. Stripped of everything – my possessions, status and appearance – I was forced to rediscover my true self and found genuine fulfilment, happiness and gratitude. I realized I had been chasing manifestations to prove myself, driven by unconscious habits of status and ego. But in that hospital bed, clad in a patient gown, separated from my belongings, my home, I recognized that my true power lay within myself: my inner strength and trust. The real value of life emerged from within. Simply, just being on this earth, filled with gratitude and love, made life worth living. This is the true essence of the Japanese concept of *ikigai* – the reason for being.

In that moment, I reprogrammed my mindset from focusing on what was lacking in my current state to recognizing what I had and feeling appreciation for everything – from my body, my family and the people around me to my ancestors, nature and the air I breathed.

Ikigai, the value of living, is not the same as having a life purpose. It is a sense of fulfilment and containment, peace and happiness that we can feel even without engaging in any particular activities or having certain belongings. This sense of fulfilment can come from just gazing at the moon and experiencing oneness by tapping into the innate power within us, using our ability to connect with divine energy – the source that we come from.

During my illness, I lost 15 per cent of my body weight, as well as essential proteins and minerals. I was unable to walk and confined to a wheelchair.

When I entered the hospital gym for my rehabilitation, I was greeted by fellow patients who were already advanced in their exercises. I couldn't even stand without support and began to cry. There were about four others in wheelchairs in the room. They joyfully came over to cheer me up. As I looked around, I realized I was the only one with both arms and legs. The others were missing limbs, yet still diligently strengthening their bodies. One of them, a Dutch man, told me with a smile that everything would be OK.

He then asked me a question: What would I like to do once I could stand and walk again? Without hesitation I said, 'I want to go for a walk with my son and my dog. I want to get back to dancing the tango. I love dancing, and I want to dance the Argentine tango again.' As I spoke, I started feeling music in my body, the sensation of movement. My spirit was dancing.

From that moment, my exercises felt like preparation for the future and a celebration of life. I felt every movement as part of a dance. I was surrounded by total strangers yet felt the sense of *nakama*, a Japanese concept similar to camaraderie – something beyond friendship, a connection deep in the spirit from a common purpose and mission, pursued with compassion, trust, protection. The energy of love and peace wrapped us together in light, transcended this physical world.

Although I didn't realize it until many years later, I was experiencing exactly the concept of *yoshuku*.

The ancient tradition of *yoshuku* is the Japanese art of manifesting. At its foundation is the expression of appreciation and gratitude, oneness with nature and an awareness that the present moment shapes the future. It is simply offering gratitude for our existence, for what is around us and what is to be brought to us. It extends beyond personal goals, encompassing people around us – family, loved ones, friends, colleagues, the community, society, the nation, nature and the entire universe.

I needed to rebuild my body — to regain both physical and mental strength — to live life fully again. I started by feeling the joy of dancing without yet dancing. Sometimes, one question by a total stranger is all we need to hear.

The day the Buddhist priest visited our family home, tears dropped from my eyes as I heard his words amid the storm. His wisdom has stayed with me — a beautiful raincoat that I can wear whenever the typhoons come. Like he suggested, I feel stronger and more compassionate since my illness. Exactly as he said, I have blossomed more than ever.

Those two months of hospitalization in Amsterdam in 2012 gave me a new perspective and a new world to live in. My suffering ended when I stopped trying to manifest goals and material desires purely for my ego. I went back to basics and bathed deeply in ancient Japanese teaching and belief. My life took a turn — and here I am.

I have found a way to navigate my life using the

essence of Japanese wisdom, which has been passed down to me from my family, my ancestors and my great teachers. Though we call it manifesting, that is not the ultimate goal. Instead, it has become my daily routine to practise my familiar Japanese customs rooted in Shinto and Shingon Buddhism, along with the traditional cultural disciplines that I learned from my mother and grandmother – the wisdom passed down the generations in the spiritual land of Wakayama. It grounds me, connects me to higher divine energies and keeps me growing as a person. It also gives me strength and the courage to act boldly and intuitively, and to make conscious choices.

Over the years, I have integrated simple, ancient Japanese wisdom into my modern way of life, wherever I am based. In this book, I invite you to explore some of the traditional customs that are integral to *yoshuku*, manifesting through appreciation and decoding the context behind these practices and this life philosophy in a manner that you can seamlessly integrate into your own daily life. With this simple, practical guide, you can learn the Japanese art of manifesting, helping you to live with connectedness, a state of flow, love, prosperity and inner peace.

Part 1

The Wisdom
of
Yoshuku

Kami
deity

Chapter 1
What is Yoshuku?

Yoshuku is the ancient Japanese custom of ceremonially celebrating in advance an important life event we wish to happen. *Yo* (予) means 'in advance' or 'pre-'; *shu-ku* (祝) means 'celebration'. Together as a term they mean 'celebration in advance'.

Yoshuku and Shinto

In recent decades, the word 'Zen' has gained popularity as a buzzword often used to signify a mindful moment. Many people in the West associate Japanese spirituality and aesthetics with Zen Buddhism, which visually is reflected in Japanese Zen gardens that represent pureness and simplicity, while some experience it through Zen meditation. However, these interpretations represent only the tip of Japanese spirituality, which is far broader than just Zen. Features of Japanese culture and the Japanese way of life have mesmerized people everywhere since our world has gone online, especially the mystic and more abstract aspects. The last thirty years of my life, lived largely in Europe, have been spent in pursuit of decoding this mysticism and bringing a greater understanding of what lies beneath ancient Japanese wisdom and the Japanese way of life.

What distinguishes Japan's cultural richness is the ancient indigenous religion and life philosophy of Shinto, which dates back to the prehistoric Jōmon period (14,000–300 BC). It is important to understand Shinto not merely as an academic pursuit, but as a living embodiment of an ancient lineage, rooted in the heart of Japan, a land steeped in spirituality and nature, where Shinto and Buddhism have been intertwined since ancient times. Shinto was already a deeply rooted part of Japanese culture when Buddhism arrived in the country in the sixth century, although they soon merged harmoniously within ancient Japanese communities.

Shinto is rooted in the belief that we coexist with countless deities, divine spirits called *kami*, which include our ancestral spirits, powerful local spirits and the spirits within nature. Shinto shares the belief of animism – that all things, both living and inanimate, have a spiritual essence. We believe our lives are supported and protected by divine energy – that we live alongside these invisible forces.

Our ancestors marked sacred locations in the mountains, lakes, fields and forests where divine energy is heightened by building Shinto shrines, each with a two-pillared wooden gate (*torii*), in these places, inviting us to tune in to the *kami*.

In Shinto, there is no founder and there is no doctrine; Shinto evolved organically. We, Japanese, tend not to describe Shinto as a 'religion', but really it is a life philosophy, a set of rituals practised in communities and families, passed down the generations, with the Shinto priest at people's local shrine leading and running the rituals and ceremonies.

To manifest a peaceful, happy, healthy, prosperous life, we recognize all that we receive from *kami*. We understand that in order to manifest what we want in life, we must express gratitude. The act of appreciation brings our vibration close to *kami* so that we can establish connections with them. In our modern Japanese society, we still actively engage in rituals and ceremonies originating from ancient Shinto practices, with our families, friends, colleagues and communities. The timeless teachings of Shinto reflect the unchanging nature of humanity, even as our society continues to evolve.

These ancient and joyful Japanese customs and traditions hold the potential to be embraced by anyone, regardless of where they live, their age or their religious background, offering a pathway towards the manifestation of a harmonious and peaceful life.

Yoshuku: Collective Manifesting Through Seasonal Celebration

The concept of *yoshuku* can be traced back to ancient Japanese spiritual and cultural traditions and forms the basis of Japanese seasonal festive celebrations. These seasonal events have been part of Shinto ceremonial rituals and practices for centuries, and to this day mark the anticipated good harvest and hoped-for good health by expressing appreciation to *kami*, the sun, nature and our ancestors at the change of each season.

The practices originate from a community-centred, agricultural life, with our ancestors expressing their feelings of gratitude for the wished-for outcome. This practice is deeply embedded in Shinto, which views life and the world as cyclical and interconnected. By expressing our appreciation

7

to *kami* and to our ancestors, and by experiencing the emotions associated with wishes, we create and engrave powerful memories and sensations within our energy field as if they have already happened. It is the energy, created in the present moment, that will manifest as our desired reality in the future.

Shinto shrines to *kami* are dotted around both urban and rural areas in Japan. While there are shared practices, including fundamental customs such as prayer, bowing, clapping and offering rice, salt and saké, each shrine often has its own, unique rituals, ceremonies and celebrative festivals specific to the *kami* to which it is devoted and to its locality. In contrast, Buddhist rituals in Japan are generally centred on ceremonies and memorial services, honouring and healing the deceased ancestors, alongside chanting, meditation and teachings, reflecting the philosophical and spiritual traditions of Buddhism.

The Shinto ceremonial festivals are particularly

enjoyed by the community, bringing people together through rituals, traditional performances of music and theatrical dance, symbolic ancient costumes, processions and the sharing of auspicious foods and offerings. These ceremonial acts are designed to bring our individual thoughts and feelings – our inner world – into alignment with our collective hopes and wishes.

By experiencing our wishes and hopes in the present moment, and collectively celebrating their fulfilment in advance, we raise the vibrations of our energy and invite our wishes and hopes for the future to remain in our energy fields. Through our seasonal *yoshuku* events, we set out our hopes and wishes collectively in order to manifest them. Then, individually, we take daily action to stay in that vibration; it is important that the act of manifesting or making a wish is not just a one-off visualization or celebration. Once we are in the flow of life-force energy, in the direction of what we want to manifest, we will make conscious choices and take actions that bring us closer to our manifestation.

Yoshuku celebrations are performed not only with family but also with people in surrounding communities and nationwide. Everyone collectively tunes in to the vibration of gratitude and joy so that the energy and the vibration we create multiply. The practices of Shinto don't mean we can banish unfavourable events, just as we cannot diminish the rain or cold of winter. However, through Shinto belief and *yoshuku* ceremonies, we cultivate power and resilience within ourselves, as well as a sense of belonging, strengthening the bond with our family, friends, community, our ancestors and the millions of *kami*. So even when a disastrous event happens, we have great resilience, which equips us to face this challenging time.

Manifesting Through Appreciation

The popularity of manifesting wishes and desires has globally spiked in recent years. We live in a world where information is at our fingertips and our desires can be fulfilled with a tap on a mobile phone. We can access information instantly, shop, find a house, buy a car, look for a new job, find a partner . . . What can we not do? Technology is advancing every day, making our world more convenient and helping many people. On the other hand, we've become so accustomed to instant gratification that our expectations for meeting our individual needs have heightened. Consequently, rather than people feeling more fulfilled, many more are suffering from depression, burn-out, and anxiety or health issues.

We all go through various phases to manifest our dreams, wishes and personal desires. We work to achieve our goals, whether that means going to university or entering a respected profession, getting married, buying a house, having children, educating those children, or going on holiday. In addition to all this, more specific desires, for material acquisition, are always being sought.

We go from one point to another, from the present moment to the future, to make ourselves happy, fulfilled and secure. However, we may never feel satisfied; we chase one dream after another.

I have experienced two different types of manifestation in my life. The first was driven by ego and personal desire (*yoku*, 欲), going from one point – the present – to another – the future – and seeing them as entirely separate; a never-ending process of trying to fill a hole in my heart. Although I manifested my desires and goals, my sense of fulfilment was temporary.

The other type of manifesting, which appeared effortlessly on my path after my illness, was different. My attention was in the present moment and my well-being was not dependant on a future outcome. It is the latter approach that is at the heart of *yoshuku*.

This Very Moment is a Blessing

The Japanese art of manifesting starts with understanding that happiness and bliss are found in the here and now. We need to let go of the thought that we will only be happy when we manifest our wishes, dreams and personal desires. Manifesting is the experience of the present moment; the formula of appreciation and healing.

At the core of Japanese life philosophy is a view of life as the experience of every moment, rather than a pursuit of achievements. Our life is a cycle, just as nature and the seasons move through their cycles, and as morning comes after night. In addition, everything has duality, two sides, like light and shadow, plus and minus. Obtaining a dream is not a purely positive experience but is accompanied by some negative aspects, and it is important to be ready to acknowledge the dualities of life and to embrace both parts as integral to the whole.

It is normal to face challenging times in our life – the key is how graciously we can navigate these periods. Even if we are suffering at the moment, there will be a positive aspect somewhere, if we look around. For example, during times of difficulty, we may still be surrounded by people who love and constantly support us. By shifting our focus onto this love and support, we bring our attention to feelings of appreciation, and the negative feelings from our suffering can ease.

We should not confuse this with positive thinking and denial, which seek to diminish the negative or the shadow side. Rather, it is about accepting that our life has two sides, and acknowledging and embracing the darkness. When we acknowledge the darkness, we can bring the light. Without noticing the darkness, we cannot switch the light on. Appreciation is the light. Appreciation brings healing, healing brings manifestation.

Some people tend to see the world more positively, while others tend to see the world more negatively; there is an art to finding the balance and keeping the equilibrium. If we are too attached to outcomes, we forget the beauty of the current moment. The key to *yoshuku* is finding the bliss and peace in the right-now.

Think about the Japanese tea ceremony, 'The Way of Tea', which centres around the preparation and serving of matcha tea. It is not just a ceremonial ritual, but an art form, a philosophy, encapsulating a way of life. For those unfamiliar with it, the Japanese tea ceremony may appear to be about the end goal of drinking tea in a traditional, peaceful setting. However, the true importance lies in every step of the ceremony and the spiritual preparation for sharing in the moment of *ichi-go ichi-e* – 'one time, one meeting' – a recognition that every moment is unrepeatable and a once-in-a-lifetime experience. The etiquette, history and principles, the immaculate attention to detail – the tea, the utensils, the kimono worn by the server, the tea bowl, the tearoom reflecting the season, and the ritual itself – all contribute to the experience. Serving and drinking the tea is just the icing on the cake. This ceremonial process, from immaculate preparation to completion, requires full attention to every detail. It is all about being in the point of zero, in harmony, in a state of equilibrium, where nothing is good or bad. I practise this state of mind every single day, saying aloud, '*Arigatō gozaim-asu*' – a *kansha* appreciation prayer that acknowledges that this very moment is a blessing. There are many things we could improve, but as we are here right now, *this* could be the happiest moment.

The Manifesting Mindset

Often, we are aware of what we wish to manifest – love, wealth, success and so on – but we are unaware of the ways our subconscious mind could be holding us back, perhaps due to limiting beliefs, fear of success, unresolved emotional trauma or a scarcity mindset. Negative emotions like these put a brake on and stop us from growing, evolving and manifesting. Imagine a tree. When the roots of the tree are healthy, the tree will grow well. But if the roots of the tree are sickly or weak, the tree will fail to thrive. It is important to be in touch with our roots, the hidden part of ourselves, part of our subconscious mind, as it is easy to become blind to any negativity we are suppressing.

In this introduction to *yoshuku*, I will share not only what *yoshuku* is and a formula for manifesting that incorporates Japanese ancient wisdom, but also how to calibrate your mindset to become the fertile ground necessary for manifesting. It is time to return to that image of the cherry blossom and the wise words of my family's Buddhist monk. Manifestation is the blossom, and you need to have stable roots to let the flower bloom. And so you must first learn how to create healthy roots for your tree.

Negai

wish

Chapter 2
Cultivating Healthy Roots

I was curious about the official definition of 'manifesting' in English. According to the *Cambridge Dictionary*, manifesting is 'the act of using methods such as visualization (= picturing something in your mind) and affirmation (= repeating positive phrases) to help you imagine achieving something, in the belief that doing so will make it more likely to happen'. Meanwhile, in the Japanese language, we use the phrase *negai o kanaeru* (願いを叶える). The Japanese kanji symbol 願い (*negai*) represents the word for a wishful idea, or prayer, that comes from deep down in our heart. It has two parts: the left part, 原, represents 'origin' or 'source'; the right part, 頁, directly means 'page' or 'sheet', but in the context of kanji it suggests 'wishful thoughts' and 'intention'. *Negai* therefore encompasses the source of our wishful thoughts and our intentions. When combined with the verb *kanaeru* (叶える), which means 'to make our dreams/ wishes come true', the phrase *negai o kanaeru* (願いを 叶える) translates to 'By manifesting our wishes, our wishes come true.' One unique thing about *negai* is that it conveys the feeling of prayer; the symbol 願 immediately suggests the feeling that we are gently knocking on the door of divine energy, sending a request to join together on a journey of manifesting with *kami*, nature, the universe and the people around us. It is a co-creation.

In comparison with *negai*, meaning 'wish', the word *yoku* (欲) means 'desire', 'craving' or 'greed'. Within a Japanese context, *negai* and *yoku* have different energetic vibrations. *Yoku* is one of the fundamental components of Buddhist teaching and of the concept of *bon nō* (煩悩), meaning 'mental affliction'.

It represents the causes of human suffering and an obstacle to living in harmony and peace. Overcoming or learning to manage our *yoku* is essential for a fulfilling life.

The kanji symbol for *yoku*, 欲, expresses a profound depth to its meaning. The left part, 谷, means 'valley', or the shape of a dent; the right part, 欠, means 'lack', 'shortage', 'absence'. The combined symbol therefore symbolizes the concept of desire as representing a state of lack or an unfilled container. It is this emptiness that triggers a desire for fulfilment, much like the way an empty stomach creates an appetite that we satisfy by eating. *Yoku* indicates the desire or need to fill what is lacking in life.

Just as the stomach will eventually become empty again, the fulfilment of desire is often temporary, leading to a continuous cycle of wanting and seeking. The character 欲 captures this fundamental human experience of longing and the endless pursuit of satisfaction, which is only ever fleeting.

There is nothing wrong with having a desire. In fact, we shouldn't deny our desires. But it is essential to ask ourselves *why* we want specific items or abundance. Many of us forget to question our desires and end up in the never-ending chase of goals, which results in the same feelings of emptiness before and after. It can appear to us that manifesting one of our desires looks like a solution to end our suffering. We will certainly feel happy when we obtain what we desire and achieve our goals – our ego will be nourished and pampered by it. But, much like eating chocolate when we are hungry, we will only feel satisfied in the moment, soon to be hungry once more. In the same way that chocolate is not a full, wholesome meal with different nutrients, the satisfaction from obtaining our desires is temporary and our feelings of unhappiness or lack persist. And so the chase never ends and we always feel something is missing – the state of fulfilment evades us.

While both *negai* (願い) and *yoku* (欲) involve

wanting something, *negai* leans more towards hope and polite requests, whereas *yoku* centres on personal desires, greed and cravings, and is a cause of suffering. *Negai* (wish) comes from a place of light, while *yoku* (desire) from a place of shadow within our inner self. Our manifesting journey will be different depending on the source of our goal: *negai* or *yoku*.

When we talk about manifesting something from a deeper, more spiritual or aspirational level, it can be not only for ourselves, but for others, too. In the Japanese language, there is no 'I' stated for the speaker of a wish, although it is implied, which results in them being less involved in the statement. This creates ambiguity, but it also gives the wish a certain power – it implies that it is not just the speaker who is making this wish, but others, too, such as family members, friends, colleagues and ancestors – possibly the entire universe is behind it. In the ancient Japanese context of manifesting, which centred around a community-based society, the involvement of family members and people in the wider community was a given.

For a healthy manifesting journey, it is important to make sure our wishes are *negai* – from a place of fulfilment – and not *yoku* – from a place of lack. This requires our heart, the container of emotion and feeling, to be filled with love and gratitude. It also requires us to change our fixed mind to a flexible one that enables us to see the world from a different angle and discover the love we have been receiving and the things that we are thankful for. Expressing gratitude sounds easy, but truly expressing it requires overcoming the feeling of lack, overcoming hidden negative emotions, and overcoming self-judgement and the victim mindset. What you wish will be the extension of what you have already in your heart and in your vibration. Therefore, your focus should be on the source, the roots, of your wish – on reaching a place of fulfilment.

Yoshuku sets us on a journey of manifesting through appreciation and gratitude along with people around us. By experiencing the feeling and emotion of our wish, *negai*, in the present moment, our *negai* will become a reality in the physical world.

Ima

now

Chapter 3
Why Pre-Celebration Brings Manifestation

Yoshuku is the practice of combining our wishes, *negai*, with a prayer of appreciation and an act of celebration, as if our wish has already been manifested in the present moment. Unlike a two-dimensional, linear timeline that prioritizes an ordered sequence of events, this approach embraces the circular and cyclical approach to time found in Eastern philosophy.

Whether we manifest our wish in physical reality in the future or not, in this moment we imagine that the state of being we wish for is here and we create a meaningful ceremony to celebrate it and express our gratitude along with the people around us. Regardless of whether our wish is physically realized, we appreciate the present moment with our cherished ones and in so doing manifest the vibrations of peace, joy, happiness and love, creating these emotions through celebration.

Tools such as visualization and meditation have their value, but *yoshuku* allows our body, soul and mind to experience the sensation of our wishes right now. This will lead to their manifestation in our physical reality, as we have already created what we want to manifest in our energy field.

Manifesting Starts from Our Inner World – the Outer World Follows

I want you to do an experiment.

Close your eyes and imagine placing a slice of lemon in your mouth. Can you feel the sourness and its sensation? Does your mouth start to salivate?

Next, imagine walking barefoot on a beautiful

sandy beach, with the warm sun shining, a soft breeze blowing, and the fragrance of the sea in the air. Can you feel the warmth and the sense of relaxation and calm?

Now, imagine walking down a staircase and suddenly falling. Do you feel your body tense up and even experience a sensation of pain?

These scenarios illustrate how we can create feelings and emotions in our minds simply by imagining experiences. If we want to feel a certain way, we can conjure it.

Typically, we believe that to feel a certain emotion, we need to experience the cause of it in the real world. While it's true we will feel the emotions during the event itself, it's also possible to have these feelings without the event occurring in the outside world, and instead just by imagining it, as we did above.

Most of us are good at worrying – thinking about events that haven't happened yet and creating anxiety and fear that can lead to suffering in the present moment. Of course, we should use feelings of worry and fear to take useful action, make plans, and help prevent future problems and create a sense of safety. By strategically using these feelings, taking preventive action can ease anxiety. You might know that Japanese people tend to be risk-averse and often worry, but we excel at meticulous preparation and planning, which helps to ease our worries.

We are all familiar with the feeling of anxiety over something that hasn't happened yet. But what about the anticipation of a happy event? How often do we allow ourselves to get excited about the future? While something may not happen, it is possible that it will happen. We look forward to events that we are certain will occur, but if they are far off, if we have doubts, or if we cannot convince ourselves they will come about, we shy away from feelings of joy and fulfilment.

The idea of celebrating our wish in advance,

or creating the feeling of the wish, might be a new concept for many and could seem odd or difficult to understand. But if you grasp the mechanism of our minds and how our brains release the chemicals associated with emotion, it makes sense. After all, we often anticipate the future when we worry or make back-up plans. By anticipating our wishes, expressing gratitude, and experiencing the feelings and emotions associated with our wishes, we create the energy that will move us towards their reality.

The Present Feeling Will Shape the Future

Imagine we are in ancient times and enjoying a bountiful harvest and general good health. With such a bumper crop, we experience joy, fulfilment and happiness, and a strengthening of the bonds within our family and community. Most importantly, we feel appreciation for the blessings we receive. In *yoshuku* ceremonies, we create this experience with family and community members, and by doing this together, the vibration of our energy intensifies. The feelings and emotions stay longer in our inner world, in our field of energy, and in our memory.

After the ceremonies, each of us embraces the feelings and emotions we have experienced, maintaining them while working towards the good harvest we have already created in our energy field. We pay extra attention to caring for the crops. Children also want to help out, which fosters their cooperation. Even though storms or tough challenges may come, people have faith and believe that they will help each other through any obstacles. The harvest will happen, as it exists in the energy field and the awareness of the people. As we embrace a circular timeline, we will hold *yoshuku* ceremonies for the harvest year after year, maintaining the feelings and emotions that an abundant harvest brings.

Now let's return to life today and imagine what *you* want to manifest. Maybe a specific amount of money, or general financial security? You might feel scared and anxious about money, believing that you will be happy and free from your worries only when you have a secure source of income or when money arrives in your bank account. So, every day, you wake up with fear and try to do everything possible to earn money all day long. You feel exhausted and your fear doesn't disappear. Your vibration and energy is diminished and it might start affecting your health and other aspects of your life. Through your hard work, you eventually earn the money you need and feel relieved for a while. But you might soon find yourself in the same situation, with money worries constantly following you. You might think, 'I thought I would feel safe when I received money, but I still feel the same!'

If we apply the *yoshuku* way, we ask ourselves how we would like to feel when we manifest that money. The feelings you wish to have might include happiness, security or calmness in the knowledge that your family is content.

First, create these feelings inside yourself by finding things you appreciate, such as your home or the bonds you have with your family, and express gratitude from the bottom of your heart – truly, expand the sense of security and abundance. If imagining these feelings is difficult, create experiences or imagine scenarios that bring these appreciative emotions into being. It could be something simple like sharing a meal with your family, and experiencing the feeling of appreciation, love and abundance. Do a quick scan of your mind. If there are any negative or judgemental thoughts, or any inner dialogue about other people or situations, write them down and set them aside.

After experiencing these positive feelings of safety, security, happiness and true appreciation, try to reconstruct these feelings, along with the vibration of your energy, as often as possible throughout the day.

Meanwhile, allocate time to work on your

financial situation. Make it visible in writing, detailing how and why you want to spend the money you'd like to have and how you will manage your finances. Make a strategic plan of tasks to receive and manage your money, complete a task every day and remain open to new opportunities.

You may be surprised by how your mindset will change, allowing you to work and plan from a place of happiness and less fear. Feeling safe, secure and confident to deal with money will encourage a positive relationship with it that will endure and grow. This happened to me, so I speak from experience.

Cyclical Time: Past, Present, Future

To understand the mechanism of *yoshuku* and manifesting, it is essential to bring your attention to the concept of time and how we relate to the past, present and future.

If you have ever practised yoga, meditation or Buddhism, you will have no doubt learned to 'stay in the present moment'. Let's ask ourselves what this really means. Truly focusing on the present moment means staying present in a state of nothingness, without our minds drifting to thoughts of the past or the future. It's about training our minds not to wander. When a thought arises, you can acknowledge it, along with the accompanying emotion, then return to the present moment.

When we think about what we want, or what we want to achieve, we often focus on the future. However, the key is to bring the energy of these wishes into the now.

In our modern society, we tend to think in a linear timeline. We can see the trails and footsteps we made in the past, but we don't see the future. We often go back to past experiences – familiar places where we can convince ourselves of certain truths about ourselves and dwell within them. Meanwhile, the future is unknown. And what about the present? Mostly, our attention is not fully in this moment, unless we are completely engaged in an activity (even a simple daily task). The past, present and future seem to be separate, and we have to walk from one point to another along the timeline.

When we feel stressed or overwhelmed, it's often because we are thinking in a linear timeline. In such moments, while allocating time for tasks, it helps to view life as a cycle and focus on the present, trusting that everything unfolds in its own time. This perspective creates more space in our minds in the present moment, allowing us to focus on our tasks without being distracted by the fear of not achieving them. As a result, we are more likely to complete our tasks more quickly and with better quality.

Think of the cherry tree: it blooms naturally, never punished for blooming late or missing a season. Similarly, when the sun rises earlier towards the summer, we adapt and get up earlier, with the world following accordingly. By shifting from a linear to a cyclical perspective, we can embrace life's flow and find peace in the present moment.

My parents always remind me that before something great happens, things often take a downturn. When times are tough, a change is on the way and it is a sign that things will turn around. It is crucial to remember this cycle and embrace the downtimes as opportunities for reflection, knowing that they precede the dawn of a new beginning for manifesting.

Ki: Beyond Time and Space

Ki 気 is an important concept that represents the idea of a life-force energy which exists within each of us. *Ki* is the by-product of our feelings and emotions. Our feelings and emotions are what we emit into the energetic field. In ancient Japanese practices, both in Shinto and in Buddhism, we take care of our *ki*, our field of energy. In Shinto, we purify our *ki* in order to connect to the divine energy around us. As with different radio frequencies, we are surrounded by different frequencies of energy – for love, peace, fear, sadness. They all exist at once in the present, past and future. You can imagine the different waves and vibrations orbiting around us. If we seek the energy of love, and if we switch on this energy field and maintain it, the future will be shaped with this energy. In this way, the present moment creates the future, with our *ki*, our force that exists beyond time and space.

We can also use this concept to help heal trauma and past wounds from here in the present moment. The events and stories of the past that we have in our memory create certain emotions, with every event having positives and negatives. We will all have experienced, at one time or another, profound sadness and pain, but while we often focus on the trauma, we can just as easily shine the spotlight on the joyful, loving moments that shaped us, at the same time as acknowledging the distress. This energy is within us and we can bring it to the surface, allowing ourselves to embody that emotion in the present moment and carrying it into our future. If we keep our focus only on sadness or anger, these emotions will define tomorrow and the day after. Our future will become the reflection of our inner world.

We can train our mind to make a conscious choice to be in this present moment and we can choose our emotions and feelings throughout the day. We can make this moment as comfortable and as beautiful as possible, and our future will follow. It is in our own hands. In *yoshuku*, we give a prayer of appreciation through celebration for the future outcome, because the future is given to us in the present.

Chikra

power

Chapter 4
The Power of Yoshuku

There are a number of Japanese concepts that particularly enhance and support the power of *yoshuku*. These concepts reflect timeless wisdom passed down through generations and are deeply rooted in Japanese culture, society and tradition. I believe they are also universally applicable and can be seamlessly integrated into anyone's lifestyle, regardless of the country you live in.

Kansha
The Power of Appreciation

Kansha means 'appreciation' in Japanese. Appreciation opens the door to bliss. When we hold the feeling of true appreciation, our hearts are filled with love, grace, fulfilment, joy and peace. Manifesting our wishes begins with appreciating what we already have. It's not about finding satisfaction in getting what we want, it is about continually filling our hearts with gratitude.

The collective prayer of appreciation is at the centre of ancient Japanese *yoshuku* practices.

Through our ceremonial rituals, we create memories and vibrations that are deeply ingrained in us. *Yoshuku* ceremonies harness the powerful energy generated collectively in the present moment and create the future with that energy. Each season, we repeat these practices to ensure this energy field remains strong.

If you are learning about Buddhism or Shinto for the first time, this may all sound too simple to satisfy your intellectual cravings, but in fact it is profoundly powerful. To feel true appreciation from the bottom of your heart is not easy. Enlightenment is right here, in this moment, whenever we truly appreciate our existence, our ancestors and everything around us. This involves purifying our inner world: moving away from the judgements and criticisms we make of others, and relinquishing the anger and resentment we have been holding on to.

It might be that you are currently unhappy with where you are in life and want things to change.

You may dislike the city or town you live in or the people you work with. We cannot change our preferences, but instead of focusing on what we dislike, we can take a moment to reflect: 'I hate this situation, but what am I learning from this?' This could be a learning point for the next phase in your life. By acknowledging what we don't like, we can gain a better understanding of what we like. Appreciating what takes us away from what, or how, we wish to be allows us to move past it, aligning our inner world with the frequency of what we do wish to be.

If we hold on to chronic anger – negative feelings towards our parents, for example, or a longing for the love we think we didn't receive as a child – these emotions can become stuck in our subconscious and in our energy field. Without realizing it, this longing for love and the accompanying anger may manifest as a sense of lack in our lives. However, when we become aware of our thought patterns, we can begin to find small things to appreciate, regardless of our past. As we gradually increase our sense of gratitude, as though turning on the light, love will appear from inside us and every aspect of our life will start to evolve. It will change our state of mind, enriching the soil of our lives from a place of desolation to one where the seeds of our dreams can grow, where beautiful flowers can blossom, where our wishes can manifest effortlessly.

Prayer, Offerings and Gift-Giving

As part of *yoshuku*, we make our wish (*negai*) with a prayer of appreciation and with symbolic offerings, thanking *kami* (divine spirits) in advance for the outcome. In *yoshuku* ceremonies and celebrations, offerings and gift-giving symbolize our expression of gratitude. Prayer, symbolic offerings and gift-giving are practices that deepen appreciation, powerfully influencing our *ki* (life-force energy) by helping to diminish negative feelings and emotions. It's like bringing light into the darkness.

When we visit a Shinto shrine, we engage in a short physical ritual of prayer, bowing, putting our hands together, clapping, ringing a bell, bowing again and giving coins. This physical act, taking a coin from our purse and placing it in a wooden offering box, materializes the communication and connection between *kami* and our inner world. This is a ritual of initiation for our wish, ingraining in our energy vibration. It's like planting a seed for a tree. The physical action looks simple but it prepares our mind and heart for manifesting.

Exchanging gifts is one of the many beautiful customs we have in Japan. It is a ritual that is integral to the expression of appreciation. At the ceremonial celebrations, often a gift is presented with beautiful wrapping. In some celebrations, it is the official etiquette to present money, in the form of newly printed banknotes in white paper wrapping decorated with *mizuhiki*, special symbolic knotting that represents harmonizing energy. The act of gift-wrapping itself carries deep meaning, as one is not only presenting a physical gift but also an offering of one's loving energy and gratitude, deepening the connection between giver and receiver.

Unki
The Power of Flow

In Japan, we hold an awareness of the unseen forces within the universe that influence and shape our lives. Regardless of who and where we are, we all possess the ability to elevate our energy frequency, aligning ourselves with the higher frequencies of love, prosperity, happiness and peace. But the opposite can also happen. We may lower our energy frequency through experiencing emotions of hatred, fear, anger and jealousy, which can lead to unfavourable life events.

Over generations, we have been taught to respect

the fact that we coexist with nature. We believe that the more harmonious our life-force energy is with nature and the universe, the more our life moves towards favourable circumstances, events and outcomes.

The symbol of *un*, 運, means 'transfer', 'movement', 'carry', as well as 'fate' or 'luck'. As you know already, *ki*, 気, is the life-force energy that flows through the universe and all living beings. Together, *unki* means the flow and state of our own life-force energy, or spiritual direction.

The flow of *ki* influences what we receive and attract. When our *unki* is elevated, we enjoy favourable circumstances, events and outcomes. When our *unki* is down, or lowered, we face challenging circumstances. Our life is a cycle and we go through both favourable and unfavourable situations.

Our *unki* is influenced by the energy of our outer world as well as that of our inner world. When our *unki* is elevated, meaning we are on a flow of divine energy and encounter a favourable outcome, we may receive a series of manifestations – not just one thing, but a holistic enhancement of our life. When our *unki* is down, we have two paths to choose from. On one, we stay on autopilot, allowing ourselves to be engulfed by fear, stress and anxiety; we fall into a victim mindset, blaming our outer world, perpetuating the downward spiral of our *unki*. On the second path, we observe the situation despite our fears and anxiety, and take back our own power, assessing our own inner and outer world and making changes to elevate our *unki*.

Manifesting is not just wishful thinking and waiting. Once we are in the vibration of what we would like to happen, we should make daily choices and take daily actions to stay in that vibration.

A key part of the practice of *yoshuku* is to raise our awareness of our daily actions and to influence our *unki* accordingly. *Yoshuku* is centred on the calibration of our *unki* through appreciation, to enhance our life in a holistic way.

En
The Power of Connection

I would like to spotlight the word *en* (縁), which represents spiritual connection. This concept is believed to influence the flow of *unki* and our journey of manifesting.

The word *en* is often accompanied by the honorific *go*, becoming *go-en*. It signifies a spiritual, mystical connection that is deeply respected within Japanese culture as an encounter guided by the universe or divine energy, and therefore beyond our control or understanding. This encounter, often unexpected, may involve a person or a place, and feels intuitively significant, suggesting that something will manifest. It is rooted in ideas of destiny or serendipity, the understanding that such an encounter was meant to happen.

When we meet someone for the first time and feel a sense of intuitive connection, or when we find ourselves in a place or country where we feel an inexplicable sense of belonging, *go-en* suggests that we are connected to this person or place by invisible threads.

This connection is like a seed. When we receive it, it's up to us to recognize it as a seed, to cherish it, water it, and let it grow and blossom without great expectations. The journey of nurturing this seed is fulfilling regardless of whether it ultimately blossoms, as it brings new dimensions to our lives.

We believe that these connections are brought to us not by our own interests or intentions, but by an invisible force – the universe or divine energy. We may not understand why we have met a person or how the relationship will develop, but we pay extra attention and express gratitude for being brought together.

It is also understood that *en* brings with it a life lesson; it is guiding us on a path of manifestation and we should be attentive. Through encountering a person or situation in life, we grow. It could be that this connection brings only favourable outcomes or manifestations in life, but it could also hail challenges. Whether positive or negative, if *en* – the encounter and connection – is impactful in our life, we must take the time to understand it. By being conscious of the lesson, we overcome it and grow as a person.

Another important concept is that of *engi* (縁起), which combines the symbols for 'spiritual, mystic connection' and 'occur'. *Engi* originates from the basic teachings of Buddhism – that our existence is supported by unknown powers, forces and blessings. *Engi* are the actions and events encountered in our lives that play a pivotal role in guiding us towards wishes and manifestations, essentially helping us to align ourselves with a higher divine energy. In essence, *engi* acts as a facilitator, pivoting the direction of our energy towards the ideal path, allowing us to flow in harmony with the forces of the universe. It acts as a supportive agent to raise our *unki*.

Through *en* and *engi*, instead of focusing on a single event to manifest, the Japanese way of manifestation emphasizes attunement to the flow of energy.

Kotodama
The Power of Words

Koto, 言, is the kanji symbol for 'say' and *dama*, 霊, means 'spirit'. *Kotodama* as a phrase stands for 'the spirit that words carry' – the power of words.

As already outlined, Shinto incorporates the belief that all things in the external world, both animate and inanimate, carry spirits. Our words are no exception, making them incredibly powerful. What we say holds immense meaning and creates vibrations and energy.

Our words influence ourselves and others. Since ancient times, our ancestors have been very careful about which words to use, especially in ceremonial celebrations. For example, during wedding ceremonies it is common practice in Japan to avoid certain words, such as 'cut' or 'break', as we want to respect and protect the sacred union of the couple. Instead, we shower the couple with the words that represent happiness, bliss, love and celebration. In *yoshuku* ceremonies and festivals, we use *kotodama*, the power of words, to uplift the vibration of the speaker and the people around us.

One of the fundamental practices in Shinto is purification. This practice helps maintain the vibration of our life-force energy, our *ki*. Purification involves not only cleansing our environment and maintaining personal hygiene but also purifying our energy field. This includes refraining from using words that hurt others, speaking ill of others and gossiping. How we use our words reflects our inner world and therefore shapes our outer world. Our thoughts, the way we think, the way we express ourselves profoundly affect our energy field and our ability to manifest what we wish.

In our daily lives, it is easy to unconsciously use words and phrases that adversely affect our vibration and energy – cursing or hurtful words, as well as negative expressions that impact other people. *Kotodama* encourages us to embrace the use of uplifting words and positive language. By appreciating the beauty and divine energy of words, we can take good care of how we speak. We can all train our mind to choose words consciously, constructing positive sentences. Just as we take care of our health by eating a good diet and avoiding junk food, so we should also be mindful of what we feed our minds by monitoring our thought patterns throughout the day and nourishing our minds with uplifting words.

We can use the power of words to create a beautiful life and peaceful world.

Sōzō
The Power of Imagination
and Creation

The word *sōzō* in Japanese can be represented in two different ways in kanji characters, and with two different meanings: 1) 想像 meaning 'imagination'; 2) 創造 meaning 'creation'. We understand from the context of the sentence whether imagination or creation is meant. From a manifestation point of view, it is particularly interesting, as both are required for manifesting.

For something to be manifested in physical reality we have to create it, and everything begins in the imagination. It is a powerful experience to imagine something without any expectations, without any attachment to a fixed outcome. But if we wish to actualize what is in our imagination, we bring our imagination to the physical act of creation – from a place of being to a place of doing.

Yoshuku ceremonies of gratitude are actualized with the force of imagination and creation. We use our power of limitless imagination to create feelings of gratitude and the conditions for manifestation. The process of *yoshuku* is in the power of imagination.

Nakama
The Power of Sharing

Nakama (仲間) is a Japanese word and concept that means a group of people who share the same purpose, vision and interests, and which create strong bonds of loyalty to each other, with mutual respect and support. It is different from friendship, although friends can be *nakama* as well. It also differs from groups that provide an elevated sense of self-identity, self-worth or social standing simply through belonging. *Nakama* is a more profound connection, a pure, true bond formed through shared purpose. The closest English word would perhaps be 'comrade'.

Nakama can be created for a short period of time, or it can last a lifetime. It can be formed by engaging in the same projects, studies, business or activitiess, such as sports, art, music, dance, culture, self-development or volunteering. These days, we could form *nakama* from a trusted online community who share the same interest.

In Japanese society, we value the sense of belonging, and nurture the spirit of the group once we are part of it. The loyalty and support established in these relationships runs very deep. I like creating this sense of *nakama* among my clients, students and followers, and also in the communities I belong to. But why is *nakama* important in *yoshuku*?

Among *nakama* we share more specific purposes or goals. We vocalize our shared dreams, express our gratitude, share laughter and joy, perhaps enjoy special meals. We can create a unique *yoshuku*, our particular prayer of appreciation, to celebrate our purpose during our shared activities or informal get-togethers. Sharing such experiences has a strengthening impact on our energy field and intensifies its vibration, which is then reflected in our outer world. *Nakama* support each other, in turn enhancing our respective manifestations through both visible and invisible forces. This is a key element of manifesting.

It's especially empowering when *nakama* also become friends. *Nakama* are the ones we can share our aspirations with, collectively strengthening our energy and vibration. Having a support group in our life journey is crucial, bringing more joy and love to our existence. It is wonderful to belong to a group, to manifest our vision, our dream, together and to nurture this wonderful feeling of community. But sometimes we may need to 'graduate' from a particular *nakama* as we go to the next phase in our own life. But this bond, the warm embrace in our heart, will remain even if we move on or take a different path.

Gyōjishoku
The Power of Symbolic Foods

In *yoshuku*, we celebrate together what we wish to be manifested. A powerful aspect of this celebration is the ritual of eating *gyōjishoku*, foods that are both auspicious and symbolic of the season, the nature of the celebration and our wishes. Traditional Japanese *yoshuku* celebrations have a profound impact on our lives because they fully engage our five senses – sight, sound, taste, smell and touch. Among these, scent and taste are especially powerful, as they can trigger vivid memories of our earliest experiences.

Eating together, sharing the joy of a meal, creates a physical and emotional experience that uplifts our *ki*, our life-force energy. Each specific food symbolizes our wishes, or *negai*, such as prosperity, health, longevity and love. When we eat these symbolic foods in a celebratory atmosphere with family, friends and *nakama*, it becomes a ritual and a powerful reminder that our wishes are already present. In our energy field, time is irrelevant – we experience the manifestation of our wishes as we eat. Just as visualizing a lemon can evoke its taste and sourness as if we are eating it, consuming these symbolic foods helps anchor our wishes in reality.

In Japanese culture, *gyōjishoku* (行事食) are special ceremonial foods shared with family, friends and the community during significant events or seasonal changes. *Gyōjishoku* not only honours the current season but also plays a vital role in enhancing our luck, *engi*, and raising our *unki*, the flow of our life-force energy. Rooted in Japanese culture, traditions and customs, and with references to Shinto and Buddhism, the ritual of sharing foods is a joyful event that strengthens family and community bonds. The beauty of it lies in creating and engraving memories via our senses, by means of exquisite presentation, the aroma and the taste of the food.

Iyashi

The Power of Healing

On the journey of self-improvement and trauma healing, it is necessary to explore what resides in our subconscious mind — our autopilot programs that control our thought patterns and our perceptions of the world and ourselves. Often, the more we search for the exact root cause of negative feelings or beliefs about ourselves, the more complex and unclear it becomes, making us feel as though true healing is slipping further away.

The Japanese concept of healing, *iyashi*, conveys a peaceful blessing — a moment when beautiful light enters our lives. It can arise at any time, even in the depths of pain or the abyss of suffering, provided we open ourselves to it.

Everyone has experienced love and compassion in some way. I don't mean romantic love, but unconditional love filled with sweetness, generosity and care – love from parents, grandparents, family members, partners, friends and *nakama*. This love transcends any boundaries. Whether giving or receiving this love, we can choose to spotlight and expand this field of love and light, instead of dwelling in darkness. We can attune to this loving energy and return to it any time. Just as we re-read our favourite books or rewatch our favourite films many times to relive the beautiful feelings they evoke, so we can revisit and expand our experiences of love and light.

Yoshuku has a healing power in our manifestation journey by creating joyful, loving experiences shared with family and friends. Celebrating through appreciation and gratitude generates uplifting vibrations, bringing love instead of fear, and light instead of darkness. This practice creates a gift not only in the physical realm but also in our energy field. Curing takes time and is often externally focused. *Iyashi* healing, however, can happen in the here and now. It begins as soon as we take hold of the autopilot programs of our mind, breaking free from ingrained patterns. It is like turning on a light when darkness falls. We cannot eliminate night; instead, we should try to embrace our shadow side while bringing light to the darkness. What matters is how much we can improve our ability to switch on the light when it is pitch black – our ability to return to the love and joy we have experienced.

When I face challenging times or feel my *unki* spiralling downward into suffering, I activate my light switch. I tap into the energy of love, drawing from my memories with all five of my senses. I look at photos, eat foods that mean something to me and surround myself with certain objects to vividly reconstruct these memories. This process guides me into a beautiful dimension of love, fulfilment, gratitude, prosperity and abundance, helping me pivot away from suffering and low-frequency energy. Instead of feeling like a victim, I express gratitude for my existence and remind myself of the love surrounding me, regardless of the situation. Riding this energy empowers me, allowing me to get back on the path of my choice and continue my journey of manifestation.

Part 2

The Practice of Yoshuku

What we nurture, we will manifest

In this section, we will explore the practical application of *yoshuku*, the Japanese art of manifesting. This holistic approach is not just about achieving specific goals or wishes but about healing and transforming your entire life, bringing peace, love and fulfilment while manifesting your deepest wishes.

My aim is to guide you in transforming your knowledge of ancient Japanese wisdom into personal experience, creating practices that you can incorporate into your daily life.

The Japanese art of manifesting is more than just visualizing and wishing for what we want. Manifestation begins in the present moment, connecting our past, present and future, filling our hearts with appreciation, peace and love. We create a fertile ground for graciously manifesting our wishes and dreams. This journey requires daily practice and individual effort, so it eventually becomes a lifestyle. True manifestation and transformation start from within, continuously elevating our life-force energy.

Let us picture a blossoming cherry tree, like the ones the monk told my family about during the typhoon. This tree has survived tough, challenging weather that has made it grow stronger, in turn producing abundant, exquisite blossoms in the spring. But that strength also depended on the nurture it received as a seed. First, the ground had to be fertile for the seed to grow, then the tree needed consistent nourishment and care so that the roots became healthy and strong, enabling the tree to withstand those harsh conditions – in doing so, the tree embodies an invigorated spirit and divine power, resulting in its beautiful flowers. These blossoms represent our wishes – our *negai* – being manifested. By tending to the tree, we ensure it thrives in all conditions and bears bountiful blooms. Similarly, what we nurture within us will manifest as our reality.

Create Your Own Yoshuku

We can create our own *yoshuku*, inspired by traditional Japanese concepts but adapted, through my practical applications, for a modern lifestyle. This method naturally evolved in my own life, leading to a miraculous transformation. I have reinterpreted what I have learned and experienced to outline the principles of *yoshuku*, guiding you step-by-step to apply them to your journey in manifesting growth and wish-fulfilment. While rooted in Japanese perspectives, the essence of this teaching is universal, and you may find parallels with your own spiritual practices.

Throughout, I will return to our cherry tree metaphor:

Life = tree

Wish = blossom

I hope you enjoy this creative process.

Outline of the Yoshuku Process

Step 1: Cultivate your wish – select the flower you want to see.

Step 2: Mind-preparation – cultivate fertile ground.

Step 3: Planning and creating your *yoshuku* celebrations:
1. Invite your family, friends, your loved ones or *nakama*.
2. Choose a theme related to the season.
3. Celebrate the wished-for outcome in the present moment.
4. Experience the flower you want to see – the wished-for outcome – with all five of your senses through seasonal foods and beverages, nature, fragrance and music.

Step 4: Daily rituals – take daily care of the tree for it to bear blossom.

Step 5: Honouring the journey – thank-you ceremony

Before You Begin

Central to the concept of *yoshuku* is the philosophy that time is cyclical, much like the recurring seasons or the alternation of day and night. The flow of energy is continuous. Just as the energy of past events influences the present moment, so the energy of the present moment shapes the future.

I always imagine different layers of vibration orbiting around us. We are at the centre and can access any layer at any time. If we have experienced a joyful and loving event, we can remember and feel it in the present, just as we can recall sad or traumatic events. Any life event that impacts our feelings and emotions can be vividly reconstructed in our minds. We can also project these feelings into the future. It's like a library: we can choose which story we want to invite into our life.

If we think of time in a purely linear way, our future, even tomorrow, is like a TV that is switched off. We are unable see anything. However, we can turn this TV on; the transmission is there, we just need to find the right channel. Much like the way the TV signal exists beyond what we see on the screen, the energy field transcends our timeline — the same vibration of energy exists in the past, present and future. If we create the energy of abundance and prosperity now, we will feel it in the future as well, and this will shape our reality. Just as the energy from the past has endured into the present — it's there when you reach for it — so it will stay for the future, if we choose to have it. We can fill ourselves with the feelings of our dreams and wishes, and create the orbit of energy now, for the future.

We often focus on past feelings and emotions, on the energy we've already created, and because it's familiar and known to us, we tend to stay in it. However, we can change this pattern and develop a new habit of energy creation. In *yoshuku*, through a process of pre-celebration and personal inauguration, we generate the feelings and emotions of our wish, our *negai*, by expressing appreciation. Seasonal *yoshuku* rituals practised in Japan are repeated every year, continually activating and maintaining this vibration in our energy field.

Embrace Your Journey

I see the *yoshuku* ceremony as an initiation, a promise to walk the path of our chosen journey with gratitude.

While it is true that we want our wishes to come to fruition, *yoshuku* encourages us to see that happiness can be attained in the present without manifestation. Often, our motivation stems from a sense of lack and desperation. It is crucial to evaluate our goals, desires and wishes carefully. Shifting our mindset from one of scarcity to one of appreciation is vital in the process of manifestation. We should ensure there are no holes in our hearts that we constantly feel the need to fill. Just as in the Japanese tea ceremony, 'The Way of Tea', where the journey is the reward and the true value lies in participating in the ceremony, we can view the journey of achieving our goals and manifesting our wishes as one continuous ceremony. *Yoshuku* is not just about a single, independent event; the value lies in the essence and practice that you take into every day.

We all have specific wishes and goals. The key to manifesting these lies in becoming the person who embodies these goals. The outcome – whether we realize our wish or achieve our goal within a certain time frame – is not the most important thing. What truly matters is the journey itself: the changes we make in our life from the moment we set our goal or wish, the daily actions we take, and the person we become along the way.

For example, if you want to be a published writer, carve out space to enjoy writing every day. If you aspire to be an artist, create art daily. If you're striving to overcome an illness, cultivate moments of peace each day. If your goal is to earn a certain amount of money, create a feeling of abundance in the present moment by appreciating what you have right now. As we engage in this process, we will find joy in what we are doing and we will become the person we aspire to be even before we achieve our goal. The moment we achieve a goal or manifest our wish brings excitement and joy, but it is momentary. When we realize the moment of manifestation is now, we can feel fulfilment in the journey. In this way, our life is transformed along the way.

The journey itself is the manifestation.

Hana

flower

Step 1: Cultivate Your Wish
Select the Flower You Want to See

Questions used for self-enquiry are powerful tools that can unveil what lies deeper within your mind. I use them both personally and professionally, especially when working with clients, helping them pave their life path, overcome inner blocks and align themselves with the energy of their wished-for outcome. In this exercise, I will guide you through a series of questions designed to help you clarify, imagine and actively shape your wish. You will experience this wish in the present moment, as if it has already manifested, shifting your mindset and creating fertile ground for your wish to take root and bloom, inviting that energy into your life right now.

The Method

In the exercises below, you will find two sets of questions. The first set is followed by answers that utilize the metaphor of the cherry tree and its blossom. By envisioning your wish in this way, you can explore what the tree needs to thrive, what challenges it may face, and how it feels when it blossoms. Manifestation, or nurturing a wish, is like encouraging a tree to blossom. Just as a flower requires the right conditions, care and patience for it to bloom, so too does a wish need attention, self-belief and perseverance.

Once you have completed the first set of questions, the second set invites you to replace the blossom with your wish and relates more practically to your life. Once you can define your wish, you can begin the *yoshuku* celebration in the next step. It is important to write your answers down. This can be done on paper or digitally.

Notice the emotions that arise as you write down your answers. Observe how the imagery influences your inner world and see if you can feel the presence of the flower you wish to see. Try to tune in to the sensations you feel in the present moment when answering the questions.

Exercise 1: The blossom

Q : What flower would you like to see in the tree?

A : *I'd like to see cherry blossom* (sakura)*, a symbol of beauty and renewal.*

Q : Can you describe it?

A : *The cherry blossom has soft, pale petals with slightly ruffled edges. It consists of clusters of delicate flowers with a subtle, blush-pink hue.*

Q : How does it feel to the touch?

A : *The petals feel velvety and delicate, like the lightest touch of silk, with a gentle, cool texture.*

Q : What kind of scent does it have?

A: *It has a faint, sweet fragrance, with floral notes and subtle hints of fruit.*

Q : What taste does it represent?

A : *Cherry blossoms represent a delicate fruity essence.*

Q : How would you like to enjoy it when it blooms?

A : *I'd like to enjoy being underneath the cherry blossom, soaking in its delicate beauty and gentle ambience.*

Q : With whom would you like to enjoy it?

A : *I'd like to enjoy it with my entire family, as well as my friends and* nakama *who have shared purpose in life.*

Q : How do you feel when you see the blossom in the tree?

A : *Seeing cherry blossom connects past, present and future, and evokes a sense of wonder, tranquillity and a deep appreciation for the fleeting nature of beauty.*

Q : When do you think you will see it?

A : *I expect late March to early April, depending on the location and climate.*

Q : What is required to see its bloom?

A : *Patience, flexibility, appreciation. We need patience and flexibility to wait for the right weather for the flowers to blossom. We need to find out where the blossom will be most abundant.*

Q : What kind of soil and environment does it need to bloom?

A : *Cherry trees thrive in well-drained soil that is rich in organic matter, with good sunlight exposure. The tree needs to be planted in a park or garden, with ample space to grow.*

Q : Can you see the beauty of the tree now, even without the flower?

A : *Yes.*

Q : What is beautiful about the tree?

A : *The energy that the tree brings to us. The leaves create beautiful shadows.*

Q : What do you appreciate about the tree?

A : *It gives me strength and a feeling of life.*

Q : What kind of challenges do you encounter while waiting for the tree to flower?

A : *The ability to see the beauty of the tree and to appreciate and love it even without its blossom.*

Q : Do you have any doubts or fears about the flowers blossoming? If so, what are they?

A : *I think it will certainly be beautiful, but I have doubt about whether my partner will like them and enjoy them with me.*

Q : What kind of daily action do you need to take to see the flowers blossom?

A : *Enjoy the tree as it is, appreciate every part of the tree and make sure the tree is healthy and not suffering.*

Exercise 2: Your wish (*negai*)

Now it's time to answer the same sort of questions for your life, replacing the blossom with your wish – your *negai*.

Q : What *wish* would you like to see/manifest in your life?

Q : Can you describe it – its colour, shape and so on?

Q : How does it feel to touch?

Q : What kind of scent best represents your wish?

Q : What taste best represents it?

Q : How do you feel when you see it in your life?

Q : How would you like to enjoy it when you manifest it?

Q : With whom would you like to enjoy it?

Q : When do you think you can see/manifest it?

Q : What is required to manifest your wish?

Q : What kind of environment does your wish need to manifest?

Q : Can you see the beauty of life now, even without it?

Q : What is beautiful about your life in this present moment?

Q : What do you appreciate about your life?

Q : What kind of challenges do you face in manifesting your wish?

Q : Do you feel any doubts or fear about your wish manifesting? If so, what are they?

Q : What kind of daily action do you need to take for your wish to manifest?

You can use these questions and your answers to make your wish more visceral and to try to embody the feeling of your wish. By using sensory elements, like colour and scent, to symbolize your wish, you can find ways to be with your wish, to keep it with you, every day.

It is normal to feel fear and doubt when manifesting a wish or starting something new, and it is important not to ignore these feelings. Instead, embrace them and acknowledge them as you write your answers. By embracing these fears and seeing what you can appreciate in the present moment, you can transform the energy of fear into courage.

Sodatsu

grow

Step 2: Mind-Preparation
Cultivate Fertile Ground

When we aim to transform our life through manifesting our wishes, we are most likely in a situation that we want to improve, or we are facing challenges or tough times. If we find ourselves in a downward spiral, we may lose our way on the manifestation journey. To realign with the state of being we wish to have, it's essential to tune in to a higher vibration. As a first step, before engaging in manifestation practices such as meditation, visualization or affirmation, it is crucial to shift our mindset via observation, self-enquiry and an understanding of what lies in our subconscious mind, to create a fertile ground for our wishes to grow.

Shift Your Mindset

While it may seem simple enough to say thank you and express gratitude, it can become difficult to find things to appreciate when we're struggling, whether it's with illness, finances or unmet desires. But we can work on this shift, step-by-step, by rephrasing our inner dialogue and how we describe our situation to ourselves and others.

When we're in a downward spiral and feeling miserable, our thoughts often turn inwards, leading to a victim mentality and thoughts like 'Poor me' or 'Why do I have to suffer?' This mindset generates negative emotions – anger, sadness, fear, hatred, guilt. When our minds are occupied with such thoughts, we become filled with negative energy, pushing ourselves further away from others and from the divine energy of the universe.

No one wants to stay in this state, but often we try to improve our situation from a place of desperation. Beginning the manifestation journey from a desperate mindset is not effective. It is important not to deny our emotions – pain is pain – but once we recognize these feelings, we can tap into our innate ability to pivot our mindset, from being self-focused to being a part of nature, the greater universe. This shift allows us to feel a profound sense of gratitude from within for simply being alive, a state of *kansha* – appreciation. We can now start to see and focus on what we have, rather than what is missing in our life. This change in perspective is essential for manifestation.

Harness *Kotodama*

In my work with clients who have experienced burnout, chronic illness or depression, and who wish to manifest a peaceful and fulfilling life, one of the first steps we take is to rephrase how they describe their situation. As I explained in Chapter 4, *kotodama* – the power of words, the language we choose – can shape the vibration we emit.

Here is a useful *kotodama* exercise. Instead of using

positive affirmations or ignoring in some other way the issues you're facing, with this activity you will reclaim your power by inviting a solution-focused mindset right now. By doing this, we actively create the future solution in the energy field and ensure the path to resolution is already set, allowing it to manifest in physical reality. This is the same, fundamental approach taken in all *yoshuku* events.

Kotodama: your weekly reflection

1. Reflect on what you have said about yourself this week, both vocalized and internal. Write down all the phrases that occur to you.
2. Notice the expressions you are using repeatedly that are negative in tone and bringing you into a downwards spiral. For example, 'I am unwell', 'I don't have money', 'I am stressed out', 'I am not good enough', 'I am a failure'.
3. Focus on the words you have used and consider how they make you feel.

- Do your words make you feel stuck and bring you down?
- Think about what you have been wanting to change in your life recently. Do these words empower you? Do they connect you to the feeling of having achieved your wished-for outcome? Or do they diminish you and make you feel further away from your goals?

4. Now let's return to our trusty metaphor of the *sakura* cherry tree, which you have so carefully planted. Imagine it standing tall with the promise of blossom. Now close your eyes and apply the words you have been using to describe yourself to your cherry-blossom tree. Imagine your harsh words as harsh weather, your negative remarks pelting the branches like hailstones; imagine your anger beating down like the relentless sun, torching and drying out the earth. How does this make

you feel towards the tree? What would you change to allow the tree to flourish?

5. We tend to be so harsh on ourselves. But if you see your beloved cherry tree suffering, what action would you take? Look at the list of words you created for Step 2. Now rewrite each of your expressions to show yourself compassion and strength, all the while holding on to the image of your cherry-blossom tree – the image of what you want its outcome to be.

Example 1

'I am burnt out and have no energy!'

This expression creates a sense of hopelessness, desperation, victimhood, despondency.

Rephrase to:

'I will prioritize taking a break, so that I can recharge.'

You admit and accept you are tired and you need rest. You acknowledge the need for, and importance of, making time for yourself. This is an expression of self-love. It opens the door to let the light in and lays the path towards healing.

Example 2

'I don't have enough money. All my friends seem to have more than me.'

Many people use this phrase without much thought, yet when we say it, it can close the doors to financial abundance. In English, the subject – 'I' in this case – is integral to the meaning of a sentence. In Japanese, however, this expression translates to 'There is no money', because the subject – such as 'I' or 'you' – is usually omitted. This makes the statement less personal, creating a sense of distance between the individual experiencing a lack of money and the object of the sentence. Create this sense of distance for yourself.

Rephrase to:

'My wallet is empty now. My wallet needs to be filled.'

I use this phrase because it's a true statement, it doesn't feel personal and it makes space for new opportunities and possibilities.

When it comes to personal finance, it's natural to focus on numbers, and when they fall out of balance, we tend to feel panicked. Of course, we need to be attentive and manage our finances carefully. But fear and panic can act as blockages to abundance and reduce our ability to recognize it. Think again of your cherry-blossom tree and what it needs to survive and flourish. It needs light, water and nutrients. Recognize what you have in your life that puts you in a position to grow and succeed. Abundance, like love, is always present.

While we may worry about our personal issues, viewing our lives from a wider, universal perspective reveals that everything aligns with natural laws. Just as life-force energy flows through our bodies to sustain us, our life circumstances are shaped by both our energy flow and the universal energy around us.

In times of hardship, we can pause, breathe, and remember we are part of this flow. Rephrasing our thoughts and words helps to balance our energy, clear mental blockages and restore the natural flow of our life force.

True self-confidence doesn't come from external achievements but from cultivating inner strength and taking control of your life. Simply rephrasing your thoughts can make a significant difference.

Take the activities outlined above into your daily life to cultivate the soil of your mindset so that the seeds of your dreams and wishes can grow and blossom. If your mind, the soil, is neglected, the seeds won't grow. They need light, water and nutrients. Only from a fertile mind and a positive field of energy can your dreams and wishes manifest.

Shuku

celebration

Step 3: Planning and Creating Your Yoshuku Celebrations

As highlighted in Chapter 1, one of the key ways *yoshuku* practices are brought into our lives in Japan is through annual seasonal festivals. The festivals, rooted in a blend of Shintoism and Buddhism, enrich our lives with appreciation that we express in celebratory rituals such as special prayers and gift-giving. In ancient times, when life was much simpler and community-based, our wishes were focused on prayers of appreciation for a strong harvest, good health and protection from plagues and natural disasters. Central to these *yoshuku* celebrations was the embracing of community and the power of collective manifestation.

Here I invite you to explore a handful of *yoshuku* celebrations. If any of the practices resonate with you, I encourage you to consider using them to create your own *yoshuku* events that fit with your own calendar and lifestyle. Celebrations shared with family and friends, as well as the wider community, allow everyone to collectively tune in to vibrations of gratitude. The energy created by each individual is multiplied and empowered through experiencing feelings of happiness, love, peace and gratitude together.

Each season provides an opportunity to focus on manifesting in different aspects of our lives. Here are some examples to get you started but you can adapt and grow your *yoshuku* practices according to what resonates with you.

Seasonal theme and aspect of life to manifest:

Spring – Health and well-being: a time for transformation and renewal.

Summer – Love and relationships: expanding love and deepening connections.

Autumn – Finance and career: harvesting achievements and honouring our efforts.

Winter – Personal growth: paving a path forward.

Wherever you live, whatever your culture and traditions, there will be national and seasonal festivals where you could add some of the concepts and principles of Japanese *yoshuku* ceremonies to expand your own celebrations, channelling the power of appreciation and collective manifestation.

Spring
Health and Well-Being:
A Time for Transformation and Renewal

The Japanese celebration we observe this season is Hanami (花見) — cherry-blossom viewing, manifesting new beginnings and opportunities.

Hanami comes from *hana* (花), meaning 'flower', and *mi* (見), meaning 'viewing', and in particular refers to the annual cherry-blossom (*sakura*) viewing, which has become such an iconic symbol of Japan. As spring approaches, anticipation builds across the entire nation for the blooming of the cherry blossom. Come the middle of March, even the weather forecast channel includes blossom-blooming predictions across Japan so that people can plan their Hanami celebrations.

Hanami dates back all the way to the eighth century and was originally celebrated to wish for an abundant harvest in the autumn by expressing gratitude to nature, the universe and *kami*. Over time, the *sakura* became the symbol of new beginnings as its blossoming coincides with a time of transition in Japan – both the new academic and fiscal years. Hanami is a period of great change and metamorphosis in families, businesses, relationships and personal lives.

During Hanami celebrations we have parties under the cherry blossom with friends, family, neighbours and colleagues, both during the day and at night. We celebrate while wishing that any changes coming our way will be positive experiences bringing prosperity and peace. At the same time, we express appreciation for our lives and having each other. Hanami also brings with it an opportunity to consider what changes we would like to see in our lives through having gratitude for what we already have. By celebrating in advance with others and showing our gratitude to the universe, we collectively connect the present moment and the future to manifest positive changes and opportunities.

Create your own yoshuku for spring

Health and well-being: A time for transformation and renewal

Spring is a season of new beginnings and opportunities. To embrace these new beginnings, we must also heal, transform and renew ourselves. Spring invites us to release the burdens of past wounds and to open ourselves up to the energy of healing. It is the perfect opportunity to express gratitude for our physical and mental well-being, honouring the health that enables us to live fully.

After a long winter, light begins to permeate our lives again, illuminating our bodies and energy fields. We can heal the broken parts of ourselves by inviting this light in. For your *yoshuku* events in spring, I suggest one of my favourite artistic healing and transformation rituals: *kintsugi* (金継ぎ), which literally means 'gold stitching' and is the Japanese art of repairing broken ceramics with lacquer, then colouring the repaired cracks with gold, to give them new life.

Kintsugi is one of my favourite workshops to give. Together, we assemble the broken pieces using a special adhesive and rub the new joins with gold powder. This compassionate process transforms something broken, and about which we cared, into something new, while highlighting the history of the broken pieces rather than disguising them. The repaired ceramic emerges healed and more beautiful than ever, with its history mapped by the scars on its surface. It becomes truly unique through this process – the only one of its kind in the world – much like our hearts.

In spring, in the blossom season, I encourage you to gather a circle of friends or family and enjoy a *kintsugi* session together. This practice nourishes our healing journey with kindness and patience, with self-compassion and the strength to move forward. Just as flowers bloom in stages throughout the spring, the broken parts of ourselves also embrace a gradual unfurling, letting go of old hurts while welcoming growth and beauty.

Summer
Love and Relationships:
Expanding Love and Deepening Connections

*The Japanese celebration we observe this season is Tanabata
(七夕) – Star Festival, manifesting love, creativity and
dreams.*

The Tanabata festival, also known as the Star Festival,
has been celebrated on 7 July in Japan since the eighth
century, though some regions also celebrate it according to the lunisolar calendar, the original method for
setting its date. Tanabata is one of the *go-sekku* festivals, which celebrate five seasonal transitions on dates
that align with auspicious numbers from the Chinese

numerology: 1/7 (January 7), 3/3 (March 3), 5/5 (May 5), 7/7 (July 7), and 9/9 (September 9), reflecting the belief that numbers influence our energy flow, which in turn affects our life events. Each *go-sekku* festival has its unique customs, with rituals to express gratitude in order to bring a good harvest, health, prosperity and happiness.

Tanabata is rooted in romantic mythology, with the beautiful tradition of sending poems and wishes to the stars. Originating from the Chinese Qixi festival, it is based on the romantic story of two lovers, Orihime (a weaver girl, symbolizing the star Vega) and Hikoboshi (a cowherder, symbolizing the star Altair), who are separated by the Milky Way. The lovers are allowed to meet only once a year, on the seventh night of the seventh month, when a bridge appears in the evening sky across the Milky Way. When introduced to Japan, the festival merged with Shinto rituals of the same season to wish for a good harvest in the autumn. These rituals included praying for summer rains to protect crops from drying out and expressing gratitude to the divine with offerings.

A key element includes the process of *tanzaku*, crafting poems, wishes and prayers. Here, wishes for improving various skills and aspects of life are written as poems on coloured paper and hung on bamboo branches along with origami decorations.

Even in modern Japan, these ancient seasonal rituals reflect the principles of Shinto and Buddhism – not as religions but as philosophies of life – and have become one of our traditions and a part of Japanese culture.

Explore dreams, wishes, love and creativity

The Tanabata festival lets us explore our dreams and wishes without holding back, allowing them to flow freely into the air, reaching the stars and universe, while celebrating an ancient eternal love story, creativity and the beauty of the universe. In the evening, families share the traditional summer dish *somen* (thin noodles in cold broth), the *gyōjisyoku* (celebratory dish) for Tanabata, while proudly gazing at the *tanzaku*, the hanging scroll where our dreams and poems are displayed, often by a balcony or in a place close to the evening sky. Tuned in to the beauty of a clear, star-filled sky, we send our wishes through creative customs, connecting with nature, the seasons and the cosmos.

This is a collective celebration and, as we celebrate together, the feeling is shared and becomes a more powerful memory. For both children and parents, it is a wonderful moment to think and talk about our dreams freely, without any judgement, to make our wishes and express gratitude in advance. Writing our dreams on colourful paper is a romantic experience, and we often practise our calligraphy skills.

Through Tanabata, we are encouraged to manifest:

Dreams and wishes

By taking a moment to be in touch with our heart, we are prompted to dream freely and explore our deepest wishes.

Love

Reminded by the romantic folklore of two lovers, we embrace the love we have and will have; we both enjoy and create the energy of love, romantic and also familial, and the love we have for our friends.

Creativity

By writing poems, practising calligraphy and making decorations, we get in touch with our creative spirit.

Create your own yoshuku for summer

Love and relationships: expanding love and deepening connections

We can use the spirit of Tanabata to nurture and deepen the love and connections in our lives, whether they're romantic relationships, marriage, friendships, family bonds or other meaningful associations. Consider organizing a *yoshuku* ceremony with family and friends to honour and appreciate these relationships.

If you are not currently in a romantic relationship, partnership or marriage, use this opportunity to cherish the love you have experienced from parents, family, friends, past relationships, or even the unconditional love of a pet.

Following the custom during Tanabata, craft your own heartfelt messages of gratitude and love in the form of a thank-you note or letter, written in a creative poetic style, to your romantic partner, best friend, a cherished sibling or parent, expressing gratitude for their love, support and the journey you share.

In addition to communicating your love and gratitude to partners, friends or family, focus on expanding the energy of love within yourself. In keeping with the Tanabata tradition, write a poem, story or note to yourself that celebrates the experiences and people who have brought love into your life. To really draw on Tanabata customs, you could use beautiful paper and transform it into origami. You can make this a shared *yoshuku* event with loved ones, together creating as many notes as you like. Whether you choose to share your writings with others or keep them private, the act of writing is itself a powerful exercise.

By appreciating the love and people already in your life, you amplify the energy of pure love within yourself. Cultivating this inner love allows it to radiate outward, filling your life with warmth, connection and joy.

Autumn
Finance and Career:
Harvesting Achievements and
Honouring Our Efforts

The Japanese celebration we observe this season is Niiname-no-Matsuri (新嘗祭) – autumn harvest, manifesting abundance.

Niiname-no-Matsuri is the Shinto harvest ritual, held annually in November – *ni-i* (新) means 'new', *na-me* (嘗) means 'taste'. It is one of the official court rituals of Japan and resonates deeply with its agrarian roots and cultural heritage. Ancient records indicate that the root of this ceremony goes back to the start of the first century AD and was performed to express gratitude for the current year's harvest, and hope and gratitude for the next.

At the heart of this ritual is the offering of the season's first harvest of rice and other produce to *kami*. In the Imperial Palace, the Emperor, in a solemn and dignified ceremony, undertakes this ritual as a prayer of appreciation for continued blessings. The Emperor's participation highlights his role as a bridge between the divine and the people, ensuring harmony and prosperity for the nation.

Above all, Niiname-no-Matsuri emphasizes a time to pause and appreciate the simple yet profound gifts of nature. It is about recognizing the efforts of those who work the land and the blessings that sustain life.

Create your own yoshuku for autumn

Finance and career: harvesting achievements and honouring our efforts

Autumn is a time of harvest, a season to receive our fruits with gratitude. In modern life, money represents the fruits of our labour, the reward we harvest. Rather than focusing on wanting more, this season invites us to express gratitude for what we already have and where we currently stand. Even if you're not fully satisfied with your current stage in life – whether in terms of your finances, career, healing or personal growth – this is a moment to appreciate all that you have and all you have experienced so far. This energy of gratitude and fulfilment can, in turn, create a powerful momentum for growth and expansion in our vibration and in our *ki*, our life-force energy.

For your autumn *yoshuku* practice, I suggest creating a *kansha* (appreciation) bowl. This ritual can be especially meaningful if shared with family or friends.

How to make a *kansha* bowl

- First, find a nice bowl or container. If you have a ceramic container repaired with *kintsugi* in the spring, this would be a beautiful and meaningful choice to connect your journey from spring to autumn – the ritual of renewal leading to the harvest – but any bowl or receptacle will do.

- Prepare small slips of beautiful paper in autumn colours – you could even use origami paper.

- Take a moment to reflect on the things you appreciate, then write each appreciation on a slip of paper, beginning each one with 'Thank you for . . .' Now fold it (either simply or as origami – a crane bird is my personal favourite) and place it in the bowl.

- Invite others to join you in creating their own *kansha* bowls, or come together to fill one communal bowl, each participant adding as many notes of appreciation as they wish. You might position your *kansha* bowl near your front door, so guests and visitors can add their own notes of appreciation as they come and go from your home. By displaying it in a special spot near your front door, it becomes an auspicious item that positively influences your personal energy flow as well.

- Whether you choose to share these notes with each other or keep them private is up to you; the act of writing and gathering these expressions of gratitude is the heart of the ritual. This simple yet powerful practice serves as a gentle reminder of the abundance already present in our lives, fostering a sense of gratitude and allowing our energy of abundance to expand.

Winter
Personal Growth:
Paving a Path Forward

The Japanese celebration we observe this season is Oshōgatsu (お正月) – New Year's Day, manifesting a fresh start with gratitude and connection.

January is a very important month for me, as it is for everyone. All around the world it is a time when many set new goals or resolutions to start afresh, regardless of cultural background.

In Japan, January holds a special meaning for laying a strong foundation for the year ahead, filled with joyful traditional customs and events. This month is brimming with the essence of *yoshuku*, and I always feel that the tone set in January shapes the entire year. The first three days of the month are called Oshōgatsu, and my grandmother used to say that the way we spend these three days will shape the path of our year, influencing aspects such as our health, relationships and prosperity. We therefore spend these days focusing on raising our *unki*, the flow of life-force energy, in every aspect of our lives. By doing so, we can guide our lives towards favourable outcomes and welcome new manifestations.

In the last week of December in Japan, we are busy closing the year through cleansing and purification practices – dusting off all the accumulated energy, and cleaning and purifying our homes, offices, cars and belongings. On the last day of the year, we visit the local shrine for purification rituals performed by a Shinto priest.

Wherever you are in the world, you will no doubt have your own special customs at this time, and in Japan our joyful tradition on New Year's Eve is to eat *soba* (buckwheat) noodles in the evening, to end the year. The long, narrow shape of the *soba* represents longevity, and it is believed that the *soba* cleanse our bodies. As we eat *soba* together, we let go of the past year and prepare to welcome a brand-new, healthy and happy new year.

At midnight, to mark the transition from the old year to the new, the bell at Buddhist temples is struck 108 times. Different sources give various reasons why this is done, but it is commonly believed to represent the number of our desires – the cause of our sufferings in our past, present and future lives. As we hear the bells from the Buddhist temples, we visit the local Shinto shrine for *hatsumōde*, the first visit of the year. It is a joyful scene as we embrace a new beginning, a new cycle filled with possibilities, opportunities and hopes, especially during Oshōgatsu, the first three days of the new year, though we also celebrate the year to come. We go to the shrine to receive blessings, express gratitude and raise our *unki*, for our health, prosperity, peace and happiness.

Shinto shrines are open to anyone, regardless of religion. We don't make specific individual wishes or desires on this occasion; instead, we connect with divine energy and express our appreciation and gratitude to *kami*, the universe, our ancestors, our family and those in our daily life for safeguarding our life journey throughout the year by ensuring our physical well-being, emotional peace, spiritual strength and harmony in our life and communities. A journey of manifestation begins by raising our own vibration and connecting with the divine energy, aligning with the vibration of our wish (*negai*).

During *hatsumōde* at any shrine, which will be filled with locals and visitors, we often meet familiar faces, exchange New Year greetings, express gratitude and look forward to maintaining supportive relationships throughout the year. It's not just about wishing each other a Happy New Year; we also energetically set the stage for our relationships and friendships to grow, wishing each other happiness for the year ahead. It is also traditional to witness the first sunrise of the year, so as to connect with the sun, the ultimate divine energy. That night, when we sleep, we have our *hatsuyume*, the first dream of the year, which is believed to deliver a special message to us.

Some people, whether individually, as a team or with *nakama*, also perform the Daruma ritual. This is a traditional Japanese practice rooted in Buddhist traditions and involves painting a single eye on a round, hollow doll known as a Daruma doll. The painting of one eye marks the setting of a goal or wish for the year, symbolizing determination and perseverance to fulfil the goal. When the goal or wish is realized, the second eye is painted, marking its fulfilment. The doll is kept for one year, serving as a reminder of the journey and helping to maintain focus. The goal and intention are also expressed through Japanese calligraphy as the first writing of the year, called *kakizome*.

At the heart of New Year celebrations in Japan is the ritual of eating certain foods. Together with family, we joyfully prepare and share the celebratory foods of *osechi-ryōri*, beautifully presented lacquered boxes filled with edibles symbolizing longevity, health, prosperity and love. This tradition completes the Japanese New Year festivities. Through all these activities and experiences, we celebrate the entire year in advance.

Create your own yoshuku for winter

Personal growth: paving a path forward

January is, universally, a time for preparing for the year ahead, setting new resolutions and defining our goals. In Japan, it is also a time to celebrate personal skills and pursuits, honouring our commitment to special activities and finding joy in personal growth.

Another meaningful tradition is to set an intention for how we want to live during the year to come. Why not create your own winter *yoshuku* with family, friends, colleagues or *nakama*? Together, you can reflect, set intentions and celebrate shared aspirations.

You can be as inventive as you like about how you go about organizing your *yoshuku* celebration. For a creative touch, identify the qualities or events you want to experience in the year ahead, such as peace, love, inspiration or fulfilment, then find the Japanese *kanji* characters for your chosen qualities and try writing them out. I often lead New Year calligraphy sessions, a common tradition of *kakizome* in Japan where participants write their chosen characters as a way to set their yearly intentions. Place this intention somewhere visible as a daily reminder of your chosen path. Allow it to guide you and become an indicator for the choices you make throughout the year. For instance, if peace is essential to you, prominently placing this word in your home may help you to choose paths that prioritize stability over challenge. If you feel ready for growth and adventure, you might set an intention around inspiration, inviting new challenges. You can choose more than one quality that resonates with you and use them as guidance throughout the year. When the wish, goal or intention is realized, it is common practice to add your signature to your word. This can be done at the end of the year as a way of reflecting and giving thanks (see Step 5).

Steps to Create Your Yoshuku Ceremony

Choose a date and time: Select a day at the beginning of the season for your *yoshuku* ceremony. If there are any festive celebrations in your culture around this time, integrate *yoshuku* principles into your event. Note that after your *yoshuku* ceremony, it is important to practise the Daily Rituals in Step 4 to maintain your energy after the emotions that the ceremony conjured, and to keep your vibrations, your *unki*, raised so that you can best navigate your life towards the state of being you wish for.

Tune in to nature and the season: Reflect on the current season, its beauty and what it signifies. Find out whether there are specific celebrations in your culture that highlight the season and integrate *yoshuku* elements.

Gather your people: Invite family, friends, colleagues, your *nakama*, in person or online, who share the same aspirations as you do. If you don't have a person you can celebrate with, *yoshuku* ceremonies can be practised alone very well. I would recommend journaling about your ceremony afterwards. Writing about it will allow you to create narratives that not only serve as a form of sharing but also make the experience more vivid and lasting in your memory.

Pick a theme, create an event: Events can be as simple as sharing a meal or something lighter, such as tea or coffee. Or you might have a festive outing, though this needn't be extravagant. If it is harvest season, take a walk together with family, friends or loved ones to appreciate the beauty and abundance of nature; if it is spring, meet up to enjoy cherry-blossom viewing or an equivalent natural spectacle.

Apply your wish: In Step 1, you defined your wish along with the colour, taste and scent that represents it. You can apply these elements to your *yoshuku* events. For example, wear the colour that represents your wish, choose the fragrance and eat the foods that summon your wish to mind. Do what you can to create the ambiance and atmosphere that you will feel should your wish manifest.

Something to taste: Prepare a special meal using seasonal produce and enjoy it with your group or alone – whatever the nature of your event, add something special for the month or season.

Imagination and creation: It is beneficial for *yoshuku* events to activate our five senses, so that our experiences become more ingrained in our memory and energy field. Imagine your dreams, desires and goals, and feel them right now. Create something to symbolize them. You can write poems, draw, sing, dance, or even just journal about them. Make a flower arrangement or cook a special meal. Use your creativity to bring the state of being you wish for into reality.

Express appreciation: Share what you are thankful for from the past month, from the present moment and the future. This can be expressed through your creativity. Make sure you verbalize your appreciation in some shape or form.

Share your wishes and intentions: Discuss and share your upcoming activities, goals and wishes, and set intentions for peace, love, fulfilment, prosperity and health for the coming month or season.

Celebrate the now and the future: Verbalize, share and explore your goals, wishes and dreams as if they are already on the way, using the list of answers you created in Step 1. Imagine how you will feel when they manifest; savour that feeling together with your group. Celebrate each other's outcomes and upcoming activities. If you share the same goals and wishes, communicate them clearly and work together constructively. Enjoy the shared journey.

By incorporating the above elements, you can create a meaningful and enriching ceremony that brings focus and positivity to each season.

Wa, Kei, Sei, Jaku

the four principles of life:

harmony, respect, purity, tranquillity

Step 4: Daily Rituals

The present moment creates our future. Manifesting our wishes and transforming our lives are the outcomes of how we spend each moment. Just as flowers bloom when the tree is healthy, so we must ensure that the tree and its roots are nurtured through the provision of light, water and nutrients in the soil. To see our wishes bloom, we need to maintain our own fertile ground and care for our own well-being. With this in mind, in addition to *yoshuku* ceremonies, it is also important to implement micro-*yoshuku* practices through daily actions designed to tune into and maintain the flow of life-force energy. Our daily routine should maintain our vibration towards our wish, our *negai*.

In this section I will share some of the daily rituals I practise, adopted from Shinto tradition and the teachings of Japanese Buddhism and ancient wisdom, which have been passed down through the generations in my family. These rituals are structured around the four principles of life: harmony, respect, purity and tranquillity, as conveyed in the timeless teachings of Sen no Rikyū, the sixteenth-century Japanese tea master and philosopher known as the father of *sadō* or *chadō* (茶道), 'The Way of Tea'. These practices can be adopted regardless of your cultural and religious background, and I hope you can incorporate them into your life.

The Four Principles of Life

The four principles of life, *wa* (harmony), *kei* (respect), *sei* (purity) and *jaku* (tranquillity) are very simple yet profoundly transformative. I first encountered them while studying with a tea master of the *Omotesenke* school, and my mother was strict in her guidance that I follow them throughout my childhood. Over time, the meaning of this teaching has deepened. Through my own journey of self-discovery, I have come to appreciate the importance of these principles and have fully integrated them into my daily life. Since doing so, I have felt a shift where my *unki*, the flow of life-force energy, has become smoother, allowing me to align with a higher vibration of energy, bringing healing, transformation and effortless manifestation along with joy and fulfilment.

This section serves as a practical guide to using these four principles to cultivate fertile ground each day, making each moment more peaceful and fulfilling. Just as flowers bloom when nurtured, your wishes, too, will bloom, leading to natural manifestation.

First, I will outline the meaning of the four

principles, before sharing some practical rituals for the morning, afternoon and evening – a method I use for myself, my clients and my students.

Wa (和) – Harmony

Everything in life has its light and shadow. I embrace both to create inner harmony.

Harmony involves aligning our inner world with the outer world, as well as living in harmony with nature and its cycles. Life has many dual aspects: light and shadow, plus and minus, positive and negative. True harmony emerges when we bring these opposing forces together, creating a state of balance. Just as nature requires both sun and rain, our lives thrive on the balance of positive and negative. When we embrace both, we accept these dual aspects as one.

Many teachings on manifestation emphasize the use of positive visualization and affirmation techniques to summon what we wish. However, deep down, we may not truly believe that what we wish for is possible to manifest and, instead, we may hold on to anger and doubt. But it is important to embrace all the feelings and emotions that we have, and to be in harmony with them by accepting them.

Nothing in life is straightforward. Even fulfilling our most precious dreams and wishes would inevitably culminate in some negative aspects. Equally, in our negative experiences, we can nearly always find a positive – a light of hope, or a lesson. It is important to acknowledge and understand this so that when we face inevitable hardship or negativity along the way of our manifestation journey, we can stay in a point of zero, between positive and negative, and be in balance.

Understanding this balance allows us to remain grounded, stable, peaceful and fulfilled in the long-term. It allows us to move forward, to achieve our goals and manifest our wishes from a state of inner harmony and peace.

Consider the relationship between our conscious

mind and our subconscious mind. Is there harmony between the impression of ourselves we give to the world and our true feelings? If there is a significant discrepancy, it can create confusion in our energy field and emotions, ultimately affecting our ability to manifest a fulfilling life.

Recognizing and resolving these inner conflicts is the first step towards creating harmony and aligning your conscious and subconscious minds. When our inner world is in harmony, our life-force energy starts flowing graciously.

Kei (敬) – Respect

Life becomes more beautiful when I choose to see what I can respect in others.

Respect goes beyond merely showing outward respect to people, objects, nature and everything around us. It is also about cultivating genuine appreciation and non-judgemental acceptance. While we might easily express respect for our parents, family, colleagues and friends, it is crucial that we reflect on our inner dialogue to ensure we're not silently judging or feeling superior to others and looking down on them.

True respect flows effortlessly, much like water, when it is accompanied by genuine appreciation. When we judge others, we often do this due to our own feelings of inadequacy or shame, and disrespecting others often mirrors a lack of respect for some aspect of ourselves. This inner judgement can create blockages in our lives, preventing us from making connections. Recognizing these feelings is an essential part of our inner work. By embracing and accepting our shadow side, which contains emotions such as shame, repressed anger, jealousy, insecurity and fear, we can dissolve these blockages, allowing our energy to flow freely and releasing our potential to flourish. To cultivate true respect and appreciation of others, we should regularly examine our inner world, catching any moments where we may think ourselves superior. Identifying and bringing aware-ness to these thoughts enables us to grow, fostering a deeper sense of respect and appreciation for both ourselves and others.

Life became more beautiful to me when I chose to see what I can respect in others, rather than focusing on their shortcomings.

Sei (清) – Purification

My outer world is the reflection of my inner world. I keep purifying my inner world.

Sei (清) is a Japanese kanji symbol that represents purity and cleanliness, while the verb *kiyomeru* (清める) means 'to purify'. Purification of both the physical and non-physical worlds is the foundation of every day for those who wish to enhance their life.

Practices such as meditation and yoga have long been known to help clear our minds for the benefit of spiritual development and well-being. However, it's also important to maintain a clear mind and purified energy throughout the day, through awareness and attention, consciously observing our own thoughts and keeping our external surroundings clean.

Let's consider our outer world. How do you view the task of cleaning? In modern society, cleaning is often seen as a low-grade task, something to be delegated to others so we can focus on more intellectual or creative activities. However, while it may seem mundane, cleaning is a sacred act.

Cleaning purifies not only our environment but also our mind and inner world. It is an act of care, respect and connection to high-frequency energy, contrasting with negative emotions like anger, hatred and greed. When we clean, both our inner and outer worlds come into harmony with purified energy.

The role of cleaning in Japanese culture

In Japan, cleaning is deeply rooted in spiritual

practices. In Buddhism, cleaning is one of the most important forms of training for mind purification and physical well-being. Monks clean daily, often polishing wooden floors with such care and attention that the task resembles a dance performance. In temples, visitors are invited not only to meditate but also to participate in cleaning tasks as part of their spiritual training. It is considered an honour to clean part of the temple and to experience the sacred energy that cleaning brings.

In Shinto, we have the concept of *kegare* (穢れ), meaning 'impurity', signalling not only a physical state but the spiritual pollution that can accumulate from negative experiences, thoughts or actions. The practice of *kiyomeru* (清める), 'purification', is essential for removing these impurities. Shinto rituals, including purification ceremonies and daily practices, focus on cleansing both the inner and outer worlds, restoring harmony and balance. Purification is not just a ritual but a way of life that helps maintain the smooth flow of energy, harmony and peace in our surroundings, spirit and our life-force energy. As we become pure, we can get closer to the divine energy, *kami*.

In the Japanese tea ceremony, the ritual begins and ends with the cleaning of the tea bowl and utensils, an act that purifies not only the objects but also the energy field around them. In schools, Japanese children are taught to clean their classrooms and school premises as part of their education. This practice teaches us to respect our environment and belongings from an early age. I recall, during my school days, that we were assigned homework to make our own cleaning towels – it was a natural part of school life.

Once we shift our beliefs about cleaning, we naturally start to appreciate those who clean our surroundings and public spaces. Simply being aware of and grateful for clean streets and buildings can transform our energy, even on difficult days.

Cleaning is an opportunity to offer loving energy

to both our outer and inner world. It is as important to our soul as meditation and yoga. Cleaning connects us to the energies of abundance, prosperity, worthiness, love, joy and bliss. It is a sacred task and an essential practice in our manifestation journey.

Jaku (寂) – Tranquillity

Stillness of mind is the most beautiful gift I can give myself.

Jaku (寂) means a state of quietness, with a deep connection to oneself. The concept is closer to stillness and tranquillity, a time for contemplation.

In the teachings of 'The Way of Tea', *jaku* represents the quieting of the mind. Just as dust settles to the floor, our inner chatter ceases, allowing us to find peace within. While mindfulness practices like meditation are important, it is equally vital to find moments throughout the day, during a coffee break or simply sitting quietly, to connect with your inner self instead of constantly occupying your mind.

Stillness is not about the absence of noise or activity. It is a state where the inner dialogue in our mind stops. In this stillness, we can truly connect with our inner self, purify our thoughts, invite respect and appreciation, recalibrate our energy and vibration, and achieve a state of being where mind and spirit are in harmony, fostering a deep connection with both ourselves and the world around us.

You may have recognized that there is much silence and stillness in the Japanese way of communication. We don't have to fill up silence with words all the time. In this silence, we can truly connect with our field of energy. To calibrate the flow of our life-force energy, this stillness, silence, is important.

Morning Rituals

Every morning is an opportunity to make the day ahead a beautiful one. Make a promise with yourself to appreciate being alive through a few simple actions that harness the power of *yoshuku*.

Wherever I am, I like to start my day with a simple yet meaningful ritual that helps me to connect with the divine energy around me and keep my life-force energy elevated. My four morning rituals follow below.

Cleaning
Ritual of purification (*sei*, 清)

Start your day by keeping your living space clean, fresh and tidy. It may seem like a simple task, but the importance of cleanliness is often under-estimated. While you may spend time on spiritual practices such as meditation and yoga, it's equally essential to give respect and appreciation to your living space and treat it like an extension of yourself.

After waking up, even in winter, I open the window and let the fresh air in. In this way, I say good morning to nature and divine energy. This morning greeting is followed by making the bed and doing a quick clean of my living space, the bathroom and kitchen area. These simple routines encourage feelings of gratitude and appreciation for everything I use, and I go into the day with this gratitude in my heart.

Not only do these routines encourage appreciation for what you have, but if your room, house and belongings are in disorder, this can disrupt your energy flow. A clean environment makes us feel good, reduces stress and can welcome the flow of *kami*, divine energy.

These small acts can transform how you feel every day, enhancing both your physical and spiritual well-being. Physical tasks can help pivot your mindset, especially if you tend to feel low or anxious on waking up. Using your body and doing some physical tasks will help you to feel a sense of achievement first thing in the morning.

Offering and Prayer
Ritual of respect (*kei*, 敬)

After greeting the fresh air and doing a quick clean of my living space, I begin my day with an offering – a candle, salt, and water or Japanese tea – alongside a prayer of gratitude for the new day. This offering symbolizes our appreciation for the abundance of food and drink that sustain our health and life.

These items help to balance my energy, representing *godai* (五大), the Japanese Five Elements of Life: Earth (地), Water (水), Fire (火), Wind (風) and Void (空). The candle (Fire) lifts my energy if I feel low or sad. Water (or tea) cleanses my inner world and calms my mind if I have too many thoughts. Salt

(Earth), a sacred item in Shinto offerings, purifies the energy around me and helps me feel grounded, connected to the earth and focused on my daily tasks. The Wind from the window carries fresh air and encourages me to greet the outside world. Altogether, I see this as a ritual that prepares me to connect with both the external world and divine energy, bringing me to a state of spaciousness in my mind, creating the Void.

I direct my gratitude towards nature, the universe or any divine presence I feel connected to. When travelling, I simplify the offering to tea or water.

Family traditions and personal adaptations

Growing up in Japan, my family had altars for both Buddhism and Shinto. Since preschool, it was my daily task to bring offerings of tea and rice to the Buddhist altar, while the Shinto altar received rice, water and salt. These practices became as routine as brushing my teeth. I would place my palms together and say, 'Thank you for today, thank you for your protection', feeling a deep connection with my ancestors and the *kami*, the divine energy.

Even now, although I don't have a grand, majestic altar at my own home, as I did in my childhood, I continue this offering of ritual and prayer wherever I am; it's not the form that matters, but the essence, and this can be carried anywhere. You, too, can incorporate a simple version of this practice into your daily life.

Creating a personal altar space

Find a peaceful spot to create a small altar. In Shinto, it is recommended you choose a bright space facing south or east, where the sun rises, and that you set your altar above eye level. Offerings can be simple – water, rice and salt, or even just a glass of water. This space will be where you quieten your mind, invite divine energy and keep your *ki*, or life-force energy, flowing.

Daily practice of gratitude and connection

Each morning, I make an offering of Japanese tea to my altar. I feel the loving energy within as I place it on the altar and say a prayer of gratitude. After breakfast, I drink the tea that I offered, which connects me to this loving energy and starts my day with peace. This practice can be adapted to any location, allowing for a consistent moment of connection with divine energy through offering and prayer, even if it is just with a glass of water.

Shifting mindsets through rituals

Performing a simple offering can help calm anxiety and provide a peaceful start to your day, shaping a more positive mindset for whatever lies ahead.

Prayer of appreciation and visualization

For your prayer of appreciation, express gratitude for being here with your wish, whether health, peace, prosperity, love or fulfilment. Create a vivid mental image of yourself in that state, using the questions and answers you created in Step 1. Close your eyes and imagine a scenario where your wish is fulfilled, using all five senses to immerse yourself in the experience.

Movement
Ritual of harmony (*wa*, 和)

In this digital era, our attention often focuses on our fingertips and mobile devices, blocking the flow of energy to our entire body. Daily exercise and conscious movement is essential to help our *ki*, our life-force energy, to flow. When we move our bodies, our life-force energy moves with us. Practices like yoga, dance, martial arts, Pilates and walking can help to remove stagnated energy and can all enhance vitality. It's great to add light movement to our morning and incorporate conscious body movement throughout the day, and it harmonizes our mind, body and soul.

Just as the words we use impact our mood, so do our movements. We can even transform our daily tasks, such as cleaning or making tea, into mindful rituals. Have you ever noticed the movements and posture of Japanese priests and monks? They are precise and deliberate, like those of the server in the Japanese tea ceremony, where every movement is mindful, intentional and like a beautiful dance.

Conscious movement and maintaining a good posture can positively affect our *ki*, our life-force energy. Movement helps us adjust our vibration and keeps our *unki* lifted, welcoming divine energy to us and keeping us on the path of manifesting, even in the most difficult situations.

Writing and Journaling
Ritual of tranquility (*jaku*, 寂)

Take a moment of stillness and silence to observe your inner world each morning. Keep a notebook and pen by your bed and, when you wake up, write down your thoughts – whatever comes to mind. There will be some days when you will feel worried and under pressure. Even if you don't talk about these feelings with anyone, confronting negative energy through journaling will help you acknowledge and process these feelings.

Understanding the Subconscious Mind

We often know what we want to manifest, but we're not always aware of what's holding us back subconsciously. Imagine a tree: when its roots are healthy, the tree thrives, but if the roots are weak, the tree struggles. It's crucial to connect with our own roots – the hidden parts of ourselves, our subconscious mind. You may be surprised at how much negativity you are suppressing. These suppressed emotions can act as brakes, hindering our growth, evolution and ability to manifest.

Acknowledging negative emotions

If you have worries, fears, anger or other negative emotions, write them down and acknowledge these feelings. You may not be able to clear them immediately, but by acknowledging their existence, you give yourself permission to release them. They will gradually decrease, similar to the feeling we experience while polishing a dusted object – it becomes clear and sparkling, bringing a sense of joy and fulfilment.

Create a 'To Be' list, manifesting through your state of being

Alongside my 'To Do' list, I also like to create a 'To Be' list. While many of us focus on getting things done, it's equally important to monitor how we want to feel. Achieving tasks can give us a sense of accomplishment, but it can also lead to exhaustion and stress. Remind yourself of how you want to *be* today: kind? Loving? Productive? Use your 'To Be' list to guide your day and link it with your 'To Do' list – preferably hand-written, as the physical act of writing sends more signals to both the body and mind. Also, ensure that your list aligns with the intentions you set for the new year, so that it will cultivate a flow of energy in your life.

Your state of being influences your vibration. If there's a specific state you wish to manifest, write it down and strive to embody it. Even if the reality isn't there yet, you can start by creating a sketch of that feeling. For example, if you wish to manifest financial well-being, identify how that would make you feel: abundant, secure, grateful and peaceful. Tune in to these feelings during your morning rituals and throughout the day, and express gratitude for being in that preferred state. Embody *yoshuku* principle.

The 'To Be' list is a creation of our manifestation. We can also create the state of being for our wish, or *negai*. By writing down our preferred state of being in the morning, it becomes more powerful and serves as a reminder to us throughout the day.

Now review the answers you prepared in Step 1. Read them through every day.

Afternoon Rituals

Every afternoon is an opportunity for creation and rejuvenation. Make a commitment to yourself to embrace the afternoon with a sense of gratitude and the principle of *yoshuku*, regardless of the day's events. You might think it's impossible to lift your spirits when you're feeling down or unwell, but I am living proof that it is achievable. With the power of *yoshuku*, it only takes a few simple actions.

No matter where I am, I like to recharge my day with simple yet meaningful rituals that help me reconnect with the divine energy around me and boost my life-force energy. Here I share the rituals I like to use and how you could incorporate them into your day wherever you are.

Intentional Speaking
Ritual of purification (*sei*, 清)

Remember the concept of *kotodama*, the power of words? Every word we use carries meaning and energy, and influences our vibration. To maintain a raised energy:

- Refrain from cursing, using harmful words, gossiping or speaking ill of others.
- Observe how you talk about yourself and your internal monologue of how you think of yourself.
- Choose language, both verbal and internal, that will take you towards your wish or preferred state.

As we learned in Part 2, Step 2, the words that we choose determine our vibration and can even direct our feelings. By consciously choosing your words, you take responsibility for what is happening, changing your state of energy towards manifesting.

Make it a habit to select your words thought-fully. It is easy to get caught up with unnecessary gossip and judgemental talk with your colleagues and friends. If you happen to find yourself in a group participating in negative talk, don't engage in the conversation and just let it pass. If you do speak up about a negative situation, rephrase the sentences in a positive, productive way that points the way towards solutions. This practice will help you stay on the right track and maintain your own uplifting energy field towards manifesting your *negai*.

Appreciation
Ritual of respect (*kei*, 敬)

Throughout the day, remember to express appreci-ation and gratitude for everything you encounter – food, water, your living and working spaces, the people around you, nature and the changing seasons. It's important to appreciate genuinely and purely from your heart, without expecting anything in return. Avoid conditional thinking such as, 'If I express appreciation, I will manifest my wishes.'

In Japan, we have a beautiful expression, '*itadakimasu*' – 'I receive with gratitude', which we say with our palms together in a prayer position, with a slight bow, before eating and drinking. After finishing a meal, we say '*gochisōsama*' – 'It was a wonderful meal.' Appreciation is essential in our lives and goes hand-in-hand with respect. When we respect what we have, appreciation comes naturally, leading to a more harmonious life.

Choosing appreciation over complaints

We can make a conscious choice to appreciate, rather than engage in meaningless complaining or judgement, even when things aren't going well or when facing challenges. For example, if you're stuck in traffic, instead of getting upset, shift your focus to find something to appreciate, like the opportunity to listen to music or learn a new language while waiting to get moving again.

When you feel sad or angry, acknowledge these emotions but then make it a habit to find something to appreciate. If things don't go as planned, instead of getting angry, stay neutral, take a moment to reflect, and thank the universe for showing you a sign. It may simply mean that there's a different path for you. Some circumstances can be extremely emotional and painful, making it hard to find gratitude. But facing these situations helps us grow stronger. Remember the words of the Buddhist monk, about typhoons and cherry blossom? Thank and embrace yourself for your resilience, and thank the divine energy and the universe for your growth.

Gratitude through visualization

In the *yoshuku* ceremony, we create our future state of being in the present moment by expressing gratitude and appreciation. Appreciation is a form of prayer, and we should consciously choose to keep expressing gratitude for our preferred state of being. Whenever you have a moment, visualize a scenario of your preferred state, vividly create a mental movie of it, and feel it deeply. Stay on track with your manifestation journey by continuously cultivating your garden for the flowers to grow.

Nature
Ritual of harmony (*wa*, 和)

Most of us spend our workdays indoors, often in office environments within urban settings. Despite this, it's important to stay connected to nature and be in harmony with it. Look for opportunities to engage with natural elements around you, even in the city – notice trees, greenery and the sky. Wherever you work or spend most of your day, keep flowers or plants and care for them. Be mindful of these natural elements and connect with them through appreciation. Tune in to the seasons that nature and the universe bring, as nature is a gateway to divine energy and embraces us with love.

Engage with the seasons by eating seasonal

produce and appreciating the current time of year. By connecting with nature, we align ourselves with the universe, attuning to divine energy and staying present in the moment.

In Japan, the location of Shinto shrines often signifies the presence of divine energy in nature. In recent years, forest bathing, or *shinrin yoku*, has gained popularity worldwide for its benefits. Whether or not you hold spiritual beliefs, being in nature – walking among trees or strolling along the beach – often brings a sense of well-being. Nature has the power to connect us with divine energy and creates space in our energy field and mind.

In our seasonal *yoshuku* ceremonies, we immerse ourselves in the connection with nature and the seasons. The energy we receive from nature is powerful, and it is important to cherish and maintain this connection daily.

Find ways to consciously connect with nature, whether through taking a walk each day, noticing the trees in your town or city, or caring for your indoor or outdoor plants at home or at work. By doing so, you can recognize and connect with the spirit of nature, which is both healing and calming to your spirit.

Stillness
Ritual of tranquillity (*jaku*, 寂)

When we have problems or issues to solve, it may seem as though we should be engaging with them all the time in order to fix them; we might feel guilty for also experiencing happiness and peace. However, this mindset does not help us manifest our wish. Similarly, while daily meditation is beneficial, if outside of your meditation practice you are constantly consumed by problems and worries, your meditation will serve little purpose in your manifesting. However, just micro-moments of stillness can help keep your vibration attuned, regardless of other distractions, so look for opportunities to create these brief pauses throughout your day.

For example, when holding a cup of coffee or tea, treat it as an opportunity to take a mental time-out, allowing yourself a moment of peace; tune in to the present moment, free your mind from thinking and let your body feel what you wish to be.

It is difficult to change your mindset when you are feeling down or unwell. But you can create a moment of stillness by changing your posture, straightening your back, raising your chin and creating a soft smile, breathing deeply in and breathing slowly out. Repeat this a few times.

If you are walking and your mind starts dwelling on problems, send your focus outward to what you see in the moment – shift your attention to the trees, plants, the sky.

Whatever is happening, it is essential to create stillness, quietness and space in our minds to keep our *unki* (life-force energy) raised, allowing us to stay on the path of manifesting our wishes.

Evening Rituals

Our evening *yoshuku* rituals should help us gradually transition from a day filled with stimulation to a state of peace. Gift yourself moments for contemplation, reflection and appreciation in stillness. This time invites deep sleep, allowing you to nurture your body, mind and soul. It's also an opportunity to reflect on your wishes and well-being.

Cleansing
Ritual of purification (*sei*, 清)

It is always important to remove stress, stimulation and any unnecessary energy accumulated throughout the day. In Japan, it is customary to do this by taking a bath each evening. This practice is a cherished part of Japanese culture, providing a ritual of purification for both body and mind, while creating time to relax at the end of the day. There are many products available to enhance the bathing experience, but I like to add just sea salt to the warm water. Sea salt helps to cleanse you of the day, both physically and in terms of any unwanted energies, promoting relaxation and preparing the mind and body for a deep, peaceful sleep. As a gift of the earth, it also helps me reconnect with the grounding energy of nature.

This ritual of purification is generally more effective in the evening. If you don't have a bath, taking a shower in the evening can also be beneficial.

Stillness
Ritual of tranquillity (*jaku*, 寂)

To close the day, it is important to clear your mind and create inner space. Avoid using electronic devices or engaging with social media, and instead bring your mind to a peaceful state.

Try this exercise: Sit quietly with your back straight and your hands resting on your lap. Close your eyes and focus on your breathing, gently inhaling and exhaling. Gradually bring your attention to your body, starting from your toes and moving up through your legs, back, spine, shoulders, arms, hands, and finally to your face, including your mouth, ears, nose, eyes and third eye (the centre of your forehead). As you breathe in, imagine golden flakes of light entering your body, illuminating every organ, and feel yourself becoming that light. Connect deeply with your entire body.

This can be done anywhere. This practice helps you connect together your body, mind, heart and spirit.

When you're in a state of calm, this exercise can be followed while imagining yourself in the state of being that you wish to achieve – whether it's wellness, overcoming depression, or any other goal. Visualize it vividly, focusing on how you would feel, what you would be doing, and expand this feeling. Express gratitude for this state of being.

Appreciation Journaling
Ritual of respect (*kei*, 敬) and harmony (*wa*, 和)

I enjoy journaling both in the morning and before bed, often combining it with meditation. Before you go to bed, write down three or four things you appreciated during your day and take a moment to reflect on how you're feeling.

Sometimes we carry worries and fears around with us all day, and we often end up sleeping with them on our minds. These worries and fears can then 'marinate' overnight, impacting our rest. By writing them down before going to bed, you acknowledge and make peace with what you're holding on to. Let these feelings rest in your notebook rather than in your mind, allowing you to release them before sleep. Then, between writing your journal and going to sleep, continue doing things you appreciate.

Journaling is also a good opportunity to review your wishes using your answers from Step 1, or to repeat that exercise. The more you engage with the vibration of your favourable outcome, the more likely you invite its manifestation. Invite the feeling of your choice into your sleep and rest together with the sense of your fulfilled outcome.

Rei
gratitude

Step 5: Honouring the Journey

When your wish begins to manifest or when you reach a milestone as part of your journey to manifesting your wish, it's important to celebrate and to express appreciation and gratitude. Even if the manifestation is not yet fully realized, take time to thank everyone involved in your journey – nature, *kami*, divine energy and, importantly, yourself. Recognize and praise your own efforts and dedication.

In Japanese culture, alongside the pre-celebration that is *yoshuku*, post-celebration is also essential in our journey. After any event involving teamwork and collaboration, regardless of whether we have experienced success, we come together with those who contributed to celebrate our path and efforts.

At the end of December, Japan enjoys a tradition of closing the year by expressing gratitude through gathering and gift-giving. We have informal get-togethers with colleagues, friends and *nakama* to thank each other, reflect on the year, and honour the shared journey and connections nurtured over time. It marks the closing of the year with gratitude and appreciation and gets us ready for the new year.

There is also *oseibo*, a more formal custom of year-end gift-giving to express gratitude to those who have supported or helped us throughout the year. The gift is usually something consumable, beautifully presented to show appreciation.

As the calendar year comes full circle, December is a meaningful closing point and the perfect time for anyone to reflect not only on what was achieved, but also on the journey itself. Even when you feel like you haven't progressed or are feeling down, this thank-you celebration will bring a sense of *iyashi* – a peaceful blessing. Your flowers may not be visible yet, but the tree knows the effort and care you've put in throughout the year, and soon the blossom will appear.

Take time to process the year's experiences and create a thank-you celebration with your *nakama*, colleagues, friends, partner and family – and, most importantly, remember to thank yourself. It's not just about celebrating the manifestations or goals achieved but the shared experiences and growth that have defined your path. This celebration is to honour the journey and the people who made it worthwhile.

How to Hold a Thank-You Celebration – Step-by-Step

1. **Share an experience:** Create a memorable atmosphere of blessing and healing by engaging in an activity you find peaceful with other people. This could be anything from attending a concert or walking in nature to taking part in a workshop or participating in cultural practices or a community event.

2. **Reflect on your journey:** Use this opportunity to discuss shared wishes and goals with the people you have brought together as well as the personal wishes you set earlier in the year, and express gratitude to one another.
   - Take a moment to acknowledge the milestones you've reached and the support of others in reaching them.

- Recognize the resilience and effort you and those around you have shown.
- Together with those who are celebrating and practising *yoshuku*, look at the kanji symbols representing your wish, goal or intention from your winter *yoshuku* practice in Step 3 and reflect on how you have lived in alignment with what you set for yourself. If you have manifested your wish or feel you have lived within your intentions, put your signature alongside your kanji symbol and thank the universe, nature, *kami* and everyone who supported you along the way.

3. **Celebrate how far you've come:** Acknowledge and honour each other's manifestations, achievements and contributions, and express gratitude for everyone's support, companionship and collective effort. Share a meal or

light refreshments featuring foods or beverages that are symbolic of this month and special to the national or local culture, like our *gyōjishoku* in Japan (see Chapter 4).

4. **Close the year with gratitude and look ahead:** Make it a ceremony to wrap up the year by exchanging small tokens of gratitude to recognize the journey you all walked, such as a thoughtful gift or a handwritten thank-you card. Share your commitment to supporting one another in the upcoming year and step into the next cycle, in the year ahead.

Let your new journey begin gently . . .

Mai
dance

Epilogue

Remember, life flows in cycles. Just as the cherry blossoms flower on the tree each spring, our wishes will manifest in the right season of our life. During our darkest moments, we may feel doubt, or even anger, because we cannot yet see the flowers of our lives. But just as a tree strengthens its roots to endure a storm, we too evolve through hardship, grief and sadness. Even without blossom, we recognize the cherry tree by its essence. It holds the divine energy that will, in time, bloom with beautiful flowers.

Similarly, we have our own essence – our life-force energy – that sustains us through even the darkest winters of our lives. This essence holds the potential for our own flowers, our wishes and dreams, to manifest when our spring arrives.

In our saddest times, the idea of 'celebration' may feel very far away. But celebration is not about the joy that comes with serving an individual interest. It's a deeper appreciation of existence, of the life force within us and all beings around us, the invisible, divine energy that supports our life, that fills us with love and light.

By expressing gratitude every day, especially during the stormy periods of life, we take a small step towards appreciating our existence. Appreciation is the nutrient that helps our wishes blossom, bringing love, peace and light even to our darkest moments.

By continually cultivating our true essence — the vibrations of peace and love within our energy field — we create the conditions for our wishes and dreams to blossom and thrive.

Now, as I keep dancing through my life, may the blossoms of your life bloom in peace.

Godai
The Five Elements of Life

Chi – Earth
With the power of Earth,
I build my foundation.
Keep me in balance.

Sui – Water
With the power of Water,
I eliminate what is not meant for me.
Keep my soul clean.

Ka – Fire
With the power of Fire,
I activate my body, my senses.
Keep my heart warm.

Fu – Wind

With the power of Wind,
I share my thoughts and feelings.
Let my soul connect.

Ku – Air

With the power of Air,
I empty my thoughts.
Open to receive.

Azumi Uchitani

Glossary

bon nō 煩悩 – The Buddhism term, meaning 'mental affliction', the cause of human suffering and an obstacle to living in harmony and peace.

en / go-en 縁・ご縁 – Spiritual mystical connection and encounter guided by the universe of divine energy.

engi 縁起 – Action and events encountered in our lives that play a pivotal role in guiding us towards wishes and manifestations, like a facilitator, pivoting the direction of our energy towards the ideal path. Supportive agent to raise our *unki*.

godai 五大 – The five great elements of life in Japanese

Buddhism, that are believed to shape our life and every-thing in the universe: *chi* 地 – earth, *su* 水 – water, *ka* 火 – fire, *fū* 風 – wind, *kū* 空 – air, void.

gyōjishoku 行事食 – Special ceremonial foods shared with family, friends and community during significant events. They are both auspicious and symbolic of the season and the nature of the celebration.

hana 花 – Flower, blossoms.

hanami 花見 – Cherry-blossom viewing.

hatsumōde 初詣 – First Shinto shrine visit of the year, to express gratitude, as a prayer, for happiness, health, pros-perity and protection for the year ahead.

ichi go ichi e 一期一会 – 'One time, one meeting': rec-ognition that every moment is unrepeatable and a once in a life time experience.

ikigai 生き甲斐 – It literally means *iki* (from the verb *ikiru* – to live) and *gai* (worth doing), translated as 'worth living'. It refers to what we value in life that brings us fulfilment and a deep appreciation for being alive.

ima 今 – Now, the present moment.

iyashi 癒し – Healing, a peaceful blessing. A moment when beautiful light enters our lives.

jaku 寂 – Tranquility, one of the four principles of life, conveyed in the teachings of Sen No Rikyū.

kakizome 書初め – The first writing of Japanese calligraphy of the year.

kami 神 – Deity, divine spirit.

kanji 漢字 – Kanji are pictographic characters originating from Chinese characters but that have evolved differently in Japan. In Japanese, there are 2,136 official kanji (known as *Jōyō* kanji 常用漢字) that are commonly used in daily life. Kanji are used alongside two sets of phonetic alphabets: hiragana and katakana.

kansha 感謝 – An expression of deep appreciation and gratitude.

kegare 穢れ – Impurity, signalling not only a physical state but the spiritual pollution that can accumulate from negative experiences, thoughts or actions.

kei 敬 – Respect, one of four principles of life, conveyed in the teachings of Sen No Rikyū.

ki 気 – Life-force energy.

kintsugi 金継ぎ – Literally means 'gold stitching', the Japanese art of repairing and transforming broken ceramics with lacquer and colouring the repaired cracks with gold to give them new life.

kiyomeru 清める – To purify, cleanse, both physically and spiritually.

mai 舞 – *Mai* describes slow, soft, deliberate and elegant body movements with an inward expression of emotion, seen in Japanese spiritual and traditional dance. There are two Japanese words that mean dance: *mai* and *odori*. *Odori*, on the other hand, refers to rhythmic body movements to music with an extrovert, outward expression, aligning with the Western concept of dance.

mizuhiki 水引 – A traditional, symbolic form of knotting used in ceremonial gift wrapping, especially for envelopes containing gift money. The shapes, number of cords and colour combinations are carefully chosen to harmonize energy and express specific intentions.

nakama 仲間 – A group of people who share the same purpose, vision and interests, and who create strong bonds of loyalty to each other, with mutual respect and support.

negai 願い – Wish, hope.

negai o kanaeru – 願いを叶える – Make wishes come true.

Niiname-no-Matsuri 新嘗の祭 – A Shinto harvest ritual held annually in November. One of the official court rituals of Japan. It resonates deeply with its agrarian roots and cultural heritage.

O-Bon お盆 – The annual ceremony to honour and heal the spirits of ancestors, which is rooted in ancient Japanese beliefs and Buddhist traditions and customs. It lasts for three days, between mid-July and mid-August, depending on the region of Japan. This tradition unites families and communities in paying respect and healing the spirits of deceased ancestors.

oseibo お歳暮 – The Japanese formal custom of year-end gift-giving to express gratitude to those who have supported or helped us throughout the year. The gift is something consumable, and beautifully presented to show appreciation.

Oshōgatsu お正月 – The New Year period in Japan, traditionally celebrated from 1 to 3 January. It is an important ceremonial holiday that celebrates the year ahead with family gatherings, which share gratitude for happiness, health and prosperity in traditional customs, such as festive foods (*osechi-ryōri*) and visiting Shinto shrines (*hatsumōde*) and ceremonial events to mark the new beginning in our life activities.

rei 礼 – The act of showing gratitude and appreciation.

sadō /chadō 茶道 – Way 道 of Tea 茶, widely translated as 'Japanese Tea Ceremony'. It is a profound ritual of mind purification and sacred hospitality through the process of making matcha tea (the green tea powder, the most premium form of Japanese tea), following the procedures, etiquettes and principles with aesthetic perfection in harmony with nature and the season. *Sadō* was perfected by the tea master and life philosopher Sen no Rikyū in the sixteenth century.

sakura 桜 – Cherry blossom, the flowers of the ornamental cherry tree.

satori 悟 – Rooted in Buddhist terminology, a realization, learning through a life experience or a state of being when we obtain a new perspective and viewpoint in life.

sei 清 – Purity, one of the four life principles of life, conveyed in the teachings of Sen No Rikyū.

Shingon Buddhism / Shingon shū 真言宗 – One of the Japanese Buddhist schools of esoteric Buddhism founded during the Heian period (794 to 1185) by Kūkai (空海, 774 to 835), also known as Kōbō Daishi. Kūkai established his teaching at Mount Kōya (Kōyasan) in Wakayama, which remains a major pilgrimage site today. Shingon Buddhism is practised through the use of mudras (hand gestures), mantras (sacred chants of Heart Sutra) and mandalas (diagrams of symbols). Central to its belief system is the worship of Dainichi Nyorai (the Great Sun), representing the cosmic Buddha with universal light and wisdom.

shinrin yoku 森林浴 – Forest bathing, immersing ourselves in the energy of trees by walking and spending some time in forests, which enhances relaxation and healing, with overall health benefits.

Shinto 神道 – The Japanese ancient indigenous religion and philosophy. Its belief dates back to the prehistoric Jōmon period (14,000 to 300 BC). Shinto is rooted in the belief that we coexist with countless deities – divine spirits called *kami* – which include our ancestral spirits, powerful local spirits and the spirits within nature. Shinto shares the belief of animism – that all things, both living and inanimate, have a spiritual essence.

shuku 祝 – Celebration.

sodatsu 育つ – Grow.

sōzō – Homophones with different kanji and meanings.

> 想像 – Imagination, an act of forming mental images and ideas, an internal process.
> 創造 – Creation, an act of realization, with an external result.

Tanabata 七夕 – Known as the Star Festival, one of the *go-sekku* (five seasonal festivals in Japan) celebrated on 7 July. It celebrates the legend of Orihime and Hikoboshi, two celestial lovers who are allowed to meet once a year, on the Milky Way. People write poems and wishes on colourful paper strips (known as *tanzaku*) and hang them on bamboo, symbolizing sending wishes to the universe.

torii 鳥居 – A two-pillared wooden gate which marks the entrance and passage to the sacred divine energy, *kami*. It leads to Shinto shrines or sacred sites.

unki 運気 – The flow and state of our own lifeforce energy or spiritual direction.

wa, kei, sei, jaku 和 敬 清 寂 – The four principles of life, *wa* – harmony, *kei* – respect, *sei* – purity, jak – tranquility, each conveyed in the timeless teachings of Sen no Rikyū, the sixteenth-century Japanese tea master and philosopher known as the father of *sadō* or *chadō* (茶道), 'The Way of Tea'.

wa 和 – Harmony, one of the four principles of life, conveyed in the teachings of Sen No Rikyū.

yoku 欲 – Personal desire, representing a state of lack, craving, greed.

yoshuku 予祝 – The ancient Japanese custom of ceremonially celebrating in advance an important life event we wish to happen, with family and the people who matter in our life.

Zen 禅 / Zen Buddhism (or Zen shu 禅宗) – Zen Buddhism is one of the Japanese Buddhist schools established during the Kamakura period (1185 to 1333). Central to this practice is meditation (known as *zazen*) and direct experiences through daily life, aiming to eliminate excessive thoughts, understand the truth of ourselves and come to a deeper realization.

Acknowledgements

In November 2023, upon leaving my corporate job, I made a spontaneous decision to dedicate four months to writing. I bought a new laptop, ready for a fresh start, and flew to Japan to celebrate the New Year – a new beginning – with my family. Somewhere above the clouds, an email arrived: 'Would you be interested in writing a book?' It was from Penguin Random House UK. And so, this journey began . . .

I would like to express my deepest gratitude to Karolina Kaim for initiating my book journey, and to Emma Henderson for walking beside me through every page with heartfelt editorial insight. To Alex Newby, thank you for your guidance with clarity and finesse, and to Nick Lowndes for the finishing touch. My sincere thanks to Daniel Bunyard and Corina Bolino for your dedication and thoughtful direction. To everyone at Penguin Random House UK, our international partners, and to Nina Shields in the US – your support has been truly inspiring and reassuring. I am deeply grateful to each of you.

To my father and mother – this book is the flower of your love. Thank you for bringing me into this world. お父様、お母様の深い愛情が美しい花になりました。心から感謝申し上げます。

To my son, Max – my greatest supporter and invaluable business partner – thank you for being by my side and growing together with me every day.

To my brother – thank you for your encouragement and support throughout my life. To my niece, nephew and sister-in-law – thank you for bringing me so much joy.

To my late grandparents, ancestors and our local Shinto shrine – thank you for the wisdom and essence of life passed down through generations.

To my Irish relatives – thank you for your warm support throughout my journey.

To my precious friends, who have supported me in so many ways throughout this writing journey – I am forever grateful.

To my dearest friends, scattered around the world – even though we are far apart, you have been the sunshine in my writing days. Thank you for being a part of my life.

To everyone who has touched my life, both professionally and personally, over the past twenty-plus years in the Netherlands, as well as in Dublin, New York and London – I am deeply grateful for your presence and loyal support.

To the members of the Japanese Wisdom Academy – thank you for your family-like bond and loving support.

To my teachers and doctors – thank you for your ongoing support, which has made the tree of my life strong and grounded.

To my grand maestros of tango – from Carlos Rivarola, who shaped the foundation, to Gabriel Missé, who carries its spirit forward – thank you for teaching me the true essence of Argentine tango and nurturing me with grace and passion throughout my journey.

Lastly, to Luke, our beloved dog and my writing companion, who became stardust as I completed this book – thank you for being by my side for thirteen years, showering me with unconditional love. You will forever remain in our hearts and in every page of this book.

And thank you, Universe, for bringing *YOSHUKU* into the world.